Author and son, Derrick

Chop Wood, Carry Water...

Listening for the Whispers

By

Michael A. Quinn

Copyright © 2004 by Michael A. Quinn

ISBN 0-7414-2006-6

Published by:

INFINITY
PUBLISHING.COM

1094 New Dehaven Street
Suite 100
West Conshohocken, PA 19428-2713
Info@buybooksontheweb.com
www.buybooksontheweb.com
Toll-free (877) BUY BOOK
Local Phone (610) 941-9999
Fax (610) 941-9959

Printed in the United States of America

Printed on Recycled Paper

Published May 2004

Chop Wood, Carry Water

The ancients tell a story of a wise and venerable teacher who was responsible for guiding his students towards the Light of Perfection.

One day a student asked, "Master, what work should an adherent perform prior to being blessed with Enlightenment?" The wise Master responded, "Chop wood, carry water."

The inquisitive student then asked, "Master, what does a perfected man do *after* attaining Enlightenment?" The Master, looking at the student with a wry smile, replied, "Chop wood, carry water."

But Listen For The Whispers

So go ahead now. Ask Me anything. Anything. I will contrive to bring you the answer. The whole universe will I use to do this. So be on the outlook.

Listen.

The words to the next song you hear. The information in the next article you read. The story line in the next movie you watch. The chance utterance of the next person you meet. Or the whisper of the next river, the next ocean, the next breeze that caresses your ear – all these devices are Mine; all these avenues are open to you if you will invite Me. I will show you then that I have always been there. All ways.

God
Conversations with God

Acknowledgements

We are reflections of the people, places, traditions and ideas that have shaped us along the way. I have been abundantly blessed by many and profoundly touched by a few who have altered my definition of reality. It is my privilege to acknowledge my debt to them.

My life took a 180° turn in 1973 with the reading of the *Science of Being and Art of Living* by Maharishi Mahesh Yogi. His book was, and still is, the most important book I've ever read. I will be eternally grateful to Maharishi for his impact on the world and me. I believe we are at least several centuries away from fully realizing the impact of his presence on mankind.

Michael and Teresa Banser, teachers of the Transcendental Meditation Program, have made an indelible and incalculable influence on my life. I love and respect them both beyond words.

I believe we find spiritual guides when we need them. Or should I say that they find us? Such is the role of Jeff Kimmel, my best friend and mentor. Thank you, Jeff, for helping to shape the journey...continually.

Acknowledging my parents represents a mere token offering towards repayment of debts that are un-payable. They gave me the greatest gifts...life and love. They gave these same precious gifts to my six brothers and two sisters. I can't imagine my life without our shared heritage.

Although Nature has painted the great design of my life, my wife Linda and my son Derrick drew the mosaic. Linda's warmth and love transcend description. She has been a steady source of comfort and inspiration. Her vivacious spirit lies everywhere between the words in this book. I'm certain our journey together will continue throughout eternity. Linda, my love and gratitude!

Derrick. I write in the Introduction… "Derrick is one of those incredible manifestations of the Creator. This book is written for him, dedicated *to* him. His mother and I have often remarked that the moment of his birth marked the first time in our lives that we experienced the true meaning of unconditional love."

To Derrick…

Introduction

The Universe is a big place. It seems to grow larger each time the Hubbell telescope transmits data back to Earth. I've always believed that such a big place must serve a big purpose. Why would God create a Universe so large that even trying to contemplate its size would send shivers up my spine? The same shivers I get when I try to contemplate eternity for more than a few moments. Never tried it? Try it. It's always been hard to grasp the notion, conjectured by some, that the Universe was created solely for the benefit of Earth's inhabitants.

However, once I dared venture beyond the view that the Big U was created for a purpose beyond the philistine convictions of some, I began asking equally perplexing questions. Such as, if we're not alone in the Universe, with whom are we sharing it? Where do they live? Do they look like us? How technologically advanced are they? Have they visited us? How can they travel such great distances? Did a Son of God save them, too? Does their history preclude multiple Saviors? How do they perceive the Creator? Could this Creator have made different rules for different civilizations, or are there natural laws equally applicable throughout the Universe?

This is the purpose of this book...to pose questions (some uncomfortable), explore alternative answers, plant small seeds of genuineness that may sprout into revealing insights into our true purpose as time travelers on our beautiful Mother Earth nestled into one of the spiral arms of the Milky Way Galaxy. I'll even suggest in these pages that the main obstacle to our uncovering and experiencing the fullness and magnificence of who we truly are...is fear. That we don't comprehend that we are literally made up of the substance of the Creator and thus it is as impossible to fear God as it is to fear oneself. And that our evolution is defined in terms of our quest to rediscover this relationship between the Creator and our own selves. I'll suggest how this fear came about, how it serves to limit our potential and how to transcend it to open vistas of incredible possibilities.

The thoughts expressed in these pages have been whirling through my head for many years. My quest for the past quarter century has focused on finding answers to puzzling, sometimes paradoxical questions. It has been an exhilarating yet sometimes frustrating journey, because each new discovery only raises more equally perplexing questions. Surprise, surprise...

However, the fundamental discovery that never waivers is the knowledge and *experience* of the existence of a unified, all-powerful, all-pervasive, unmanifested and unchanging field of existence at the foundation of all existence. Mystics from most religious traditions have experientially understood this reality. And, today's quantum physicists are lending scientific validity to its existence. It is given many names...the Unified Field, Being, the Absolute are but a few. But, its fundamental characteristics are the same. And, most importantly, this silent, unmanifested field, the basis of all creation, the well-spring of all that is, can be *experienced* at its source and assimilated into every moment of our lives, giving true meaning to that perpetually evasive term "enlightenment."

As I said, this is an ongoing quest. Experience begets experience. But why a book?

Joseph Campbell, preeminent scholar, authority on mythology, once defined two types of heroic deeds. One, he said, is the physical deed, in which the "hero performs a courageous act in battle or saves a life." The other kind is a spiritual deed, in which the "hero learns to experience the supernormal range of human life and then comes back with a message." My hunger to form a message based on my knowledge and experience consumes me. The vehicle to express this message is this book. The catalyst for my *need* to express it is Derrick, my son.

Derrick is one of those incredible manifestations of the Creator. The moment of his birth was, and still is, the most extraordinary, exhilarating, blissful, and heart-expanding experience of my life. This book is written for him, dedicated *to* him. And as his mother Linda and I have often remarked, mere words could never, ever completely explain the impact he has had on our lives. For the first time in our lives, we both experienced the true meaning of unconditional love.

I love you, Derrick.

My journey towards enlightenment is my legacy to Derrick. I don't have the acumen to teach him how to repair cars, tie fishing lures or explain baseball's infield fly rule. But I can share my quest with him, both my knowledge and, more importantly, by example. It is my most fervent prayer that my thoughts expressed in these pages will touch him at a fundamental level, empowering him to both cherish and honor this work. And my most burning wish is that he is able to assimilate this knowledge in a manner that will awaken him to his own enlightenment.

To tell the truth, I've been in mourning for this boy, or for whatever corner of my heart died when this child and his magical childhood slid out of my arms, never to ride on my shoulders again.

This book is written in a conversational style, with short chapters focusing on specific themes. It is certainly *not* meant to be a scholarly work. I'm providing only the most cursory of insights into subjects that have consumed minds far more developed than mine. I'm simply offering a few keys for raising one's awareness…a personal road map for achieving spiritual clarity.

As I write, I've tried to imagine that I'm talking directly to you, without sounding like a pontifical fool. I hope this style doesn't detract from the depth of the information. I want you to *enjoy* this material. I thoroughly enjoyed writing it. I hope I'm successful in conveying to you some of my excitement. (Chapter 1 alone is worth the price of the book. I *guarantee* that you'll never look at the nighttime sky in the same way again!)

We are rapidly advancing as a technical society, unlocking secrets from the finest elementary particles to what happened after the first trillionth of a trillionth of a trillionth of a second after the Big Bang. (Books have been written about what occurred in this infinitesimal genesis moment!) And yet, I often feel as though we've only taken the first, miniscule steps forward from our Neanderthal ancestry compared with the knowledge and advances that will manifest in the centuries to come.

The book is divided into two sections.

Section I: The Awakening: Tries to connect the dots between the size of the Universe and the countless self-aware beings of countless civilizations living in it, with challenging concepts suggesting that we have the ability to almost instantaneously connect with any point in time and space *in* this unfathomable Universe. Subsequent chapters in this section try to quantify the ability of the Universe's beings to tap directly into and experience the magnificent energy that creates and powers the Universe...the Creator's Love; how to spontaneously assimilate the Creator's energy (Love) in a manner that engenders spontaneous right action, while simultaneously creating a field that radiates this energy in a manner that contributes significantly to humanity's quint-essential quest for peace; and to *experience* first-hand the true significance of having been created in the image and likeness of the Creator. I know that's a mouthful. But hey, the subject matter isn't exactly chopped liver. We're talking here about all the marbles! I love it...

Section II: The Journey Continues: These chapters simply reflect my points of view on religious and spiritual subjects that I find especially intriguing, although the subject matter does have a kindred relationship to the thoughts expressed in Section I.

The heart of this book focuses on the transcendent nature of life. I'll define this term as we go along. However, suffice to say here that most of humankind, despite our technological and sociological advances, has been stymied by the belief that we exist and function separately from each other and from our Creator. The wall created by this entrenched belief has been translated into a myriad of societal and personal ills, and prevents us from functioning *spontaneously* from the pure and profoundly powerful level of the finest relative aspect of creation that always results in correct thought and behavior.

And the most unfortunate and tragic consequence of this separation is the belief that we have been disenfranchised from the Creator. This belief has generated a "Him versus us" mentality, often overshadowed by the *fear* that He constantly sits in judgment, waiting to chastise us when we fail to adhere to His word.

There are remedies for this dilemma, based not on intellectual query, but rather on experiential, first-hand assimilation of the transcendent values of the Creator's Love. We'll discuss these remedies.

Please indulge me if at times I sound "preachy," especially when writing about the historical impact of traditional religious thought on mankind. *I unequivocally recognize that your beliefs are very precious to you.* My only intention is to create a "whisper" in your heart, a gentle "breath of possibility" that deeper truths may be resting under the canopy of institutional religion. If you can allow yourself to listen to these whispers, without *fear*, you may come to directly *experience* more of the Creator's Love that permeates every belief system.

It is my profoundest wish that these whispers resonate at the deepest level of your awareness. That if you're ready for change from unfulfilling, culturally conditioned life patterns, the whispers will fan the flames of expanded states of consciousness that place you on a path to self-realization.

It is important to stay true to our values, for these are the values of our parents, of our parent's parents, of our friends and of society. They form the structure of our life, and to lose them would be to unravel the fabric of our experience. Still, try to examine the ideas herein one by one. Don't dismantle the house, but look at each brick, and replace those that appear broken, which no longer support the structure.

I'm reminded here of a quote, from a source that escapes me, that "many religious people prefer certainty to truth." If this assertion causes you to twitch a little, listen for the whispers as you read. They're real. They won't yell at you. For just a few moments, try to suspend your beliefs and entertain the possibility that God wants you to discover even *more* about Him, and that there is absolutely nothing to fear by listening to the whispers with your *heart* rather than your mind. "Hear God on the whisper! Don't wait for the earthquake!"

The willingness to trust and live with your own experience, regardless of who else agrees or disagrees...*that* becomes the key to your identity.

Finally, during the span of years devoted to putting these thoughts to words, I was constantly dogged by the rather well known and penetrating encounter of the 11th century's Thomas Aquinas. Aquinas was a prolific theological author. He worked for years on his theological masterpiece, the *Summa Theologica*, only to refuse to finish the work after experiencing a profound mystical experience shortly before his death. Aquanis stated that his vision affected him so profoundly that "I cannot go on. All that I have written seems to me like so much straw compared to what I have seen and what has been revealed to me."

Actually, my ultimate quest *is* to eventually experience the knowledge in this book and all my intellectual inquiry as simply "straw." Then I'll know that I'm getting close.

Table of Contents

Section I:
The Awakening

Chapter 1: The Great Designer

> I'm astounded by people who want to "know" the universe when it's hard enough to find your way around Chinatown.
>
> Woody Allen

> Think of the rivers of blood spilled by all the generals and emperors so that, in glory and triumph, they could become the momentary master of a fraction of a dot.
>
> > Carl Sagan, reflecting on the last photo taken by *Voyager 1* as it exited the solar system in 1990, depicting the Earth as a mere pixel of light.

The Creator has created a magnificent, almost undefinable Universe whose boundaries are unknown to man. A Universe so boundless, teeming with countless billions of galaxies, containing trillions of star systems, which in turn claim heritage to trillions of planets.

Oh, I know. At this point in time, astronomers have only been able to validate the existence of a handful of planets. But this discussion isn't about scientific validation. I'm speaking to your intuitive, right brain hemisphere. The brain hemisphere that says if astronomers have found at least 120 *billion* galaxies, that it's reasonable to assume that each of those galaxies support more than a handful of planets. Makes sense, doesn't it?

So, how big *is* it? It's beyond human understanding. When we ponder an enchanting nighttime sky abounding with countless stars, we usually take a deep breath and acknowledge the vastness and majesty of it all...and generally leave it at that. The late astronomer Carl Sagan writes that the nighttime sky "is a profound sermon on humility."

From a source I can't locate, the author eloquently writes that "All the great religions have a place for awe, for ecstatic transport at the wonder and beauty of creation. And it's exactly this feeling of spine-tingling, breath-catching awe…almost worship…this flooding the chest with ecstatic wonder, that looking at the heavens can provide. And it does so beyond the wildest dreams of saints and mystics. The merest glance through a telescope at a long-ago galaxy of a billion worlds, is enough to render parochial the very psalms of praise."

The dimensions of the Universe are so large that using familiar units of distance make little sense. Instead, we measure distance by the speed of light years. One light year is equal to the distance traveled by light in one Earth year, or about six *trillion* miles. The closest star to earth, Proxima Centauri, is 25 trillion miles away, or 4.2 light years.

As we said, there are an estimated 120 billion galaxies. Our Milky Way Galaxy is one of them. How big is *our* Galaxy? There are an estimated 200 billion star systems in the Milky Way…but my eyes start to glaze over when numbers go past six zeros.

To help put this size into perspective, suppose that you and your significant other were to take a starship cruise across the Galaxy. (You wouldn't want to go that far *alone*, would you?). Of course, you'll be traveling at the speed of light, or 186,000 miles a *second*. This speed is equivalent to circling the Earth almost eight times in just one second. We just learned that light travels about six trillion miles in one year. And the Milky Way is about 120,000 light years in diameter. Therefore, your trip will cover six trillion miles times 120,000 years or 720,000,000,000,000,000 miles…that's 720 followed by 15 zeros!

If you started your 120,000-year trip when the two-mile deep Greenland ice sheet started forming about 110,000 years ago, you would *still* have about 10,000 years to go. And after 120,000 years, you would have only traveled across the diameter of *one* average-size galaxy, one of 120 billion! (We'll conveniently ignore for the moment Einstein's Theory of Special Relativity that states that the passage of time slows down to almost zilch as you approach the speed of light. I'm more interested in making a point about size.)

Here is another example of the size of the Milky Way and the *speed* at which we're all traveling around the Galaxy.

While you're sipping your morning coffee and reading the newspaper and wondering if the last occupant of the bathroom left you any hot water, you hardly notice that the Earth, and thus *you*, is spinning at a healthy 1,041 miles per hour. Nor will you notice that by the time you finish your shower, get dressed and finish your ten-mile drive to work, you will have traveled as a passenger on planet Earth about *67,000 miles* through outer space, orbiting the Sun.

But hold on. While you're gingerly orbiting the Sun at 67,000 mph, the Sun is orbiting the Galaxy at a whopping speed of 135 miles per *second*, carrying us and the entire solar system along with it. But even at this meteoric speed, it will take the solar system 226 *million* Earth years to complete just *one* orbit of the Galaxy. So don't be in a big hurry to finish that cup of coffee…time is on your side!

Now, tighten your cosmic seatbelt while we venture into the incredible realm of the space *between* galaxies.

Galaxies are not randomly distributed throughout the Universe. Rather, they exist in clusters or clumps. This clumpiness poses one of the thorniest puzzles in cosmology, having something to do with dark matter, cosmic strings, and the Big Bang.

The distance between these galactic clumps can be as many as several hundred million light years. This distance makes your trip of 120,000 light years equivalent to a trip to the corner galactic grocery!

Here is another example that demonstrates this stratospheric distance.

Imagine reading in your morning newspaper this extraordinary headline. "Milky Way and Andromeda Galaxies on Collision Course!" The article explains that the Milky Way Galaxy and our nearest galactic neighbor, Andromeda, are speeding towards each other at *300,000* miles an hour! Yipes!

However, at the end of the article, you read that at this speed, it will take about 2 *billion* years before massive gravitational effects start tearing apart the spiral arms of the Milky Way in advance of a major collision between the two galaxies. Distance becomes our savior! (But if you're still concerned, don't be. In just a billion years, the Sun's conversion of hydrogen to helium will create a tremendous increase in solar heat, melting the polar icecaps and evaporating the oceans, making the Earth unlivable. I hope you feel better now.)

The galactic clump that includes the Milky Way is called the Coma Cluster of galaxies. While all this motion of the Earth, the Sun and the galaxies within the Cluster is occurring, the Coma Cluster is spinning away from its closest neighboring galaxy cluster at a speed of 7,000 kilometers per second! This is the motion called the expansion of the Universe that derives from the Big Bang.

Here is another startling figure to substantiate the vastness of space. If we were to randomly insert you into the Universe, the chance that you would find yourself on or near a planet would be less than one in a billion trillion trillion (10^{-33}), a one followed by 33 zeros, or...

$$1,000,000,000,000,000,000,000,000,000,000,000$$

This is because outer space is mostly, well, …space. It's empty. The Universe contains only one atom for every 88 gallons of space. That's a lot of space!

Yet what is even more awe-inspiring is the infinity of space itself, the depth and stillness that allows all of that magnificence to be. Nothing could be more awe-inspiring and majestic than the inconceivable vastness and stillness of space, and yet what is it? Emptiness, vast emptiness.

As we said, our Milky Way Galaxy has as many as 200 billion stars and, in all galaxies, there are perhaps as many planets as stars, according to Carl Sagan. This translates to $10 \times 10^9 \times 10^{12} = 10^{22}$, or 10 billion trillion planets! There go those glazed eyes again…

Does the Universe have a limit, or does it go on forever? It's one of science's most perplexing questions, involving, at a minimum, Hawking's concept of imaginary time versus real time, Feyman's "sum over histories" theory, and assorted "anthropic" principles. And I wouldn't even *think* of trying to explain them.

However, despite the scientific voodoo, there is general agreement on one basic tenet. The Universe is generally considered to be finite in space, although this space evidently doesn't have any boundaries. Gravity is apparently so strong that space *folds* onto itself, making it like the surface of the Earth. If you traveled in a certain direction on the Earth's surface, you would never fall over the edge. You would eventually return to where you started.

Now, let's add *another* intriguing twist to this "how big is it" scenario.

It's perplexing enough trying to conceptualize the size of the Universe. But we have to also remember that everything we observe in the Universe belongs to the *past*. It's an illusion.

In the heavenly vault we observe on a starry night, there are many stars that are already extinct. Their light may have been extinguished millions of years ago. Our perception of them is due to the light-years it takes for those images to reach our eyes. Even our Sun, a mere 93 million miles away, which provides us with nostalgic sunsets as it sits on the rim of the horizon each evening, is in reality just the *phantom* of a star that already set eight minutes ago.

Now here's something fun to think about. If a super powerful telescope existed on a distant planet 2,000 light-years away from Earth, the use of this telescope would allow an observer on that planet to witness historic events that happened here on Earth 2,000 years ago *as they were occurring in real time.* The observer might *literally* see Jesus of Nazareth delivering the Sermon on the Mount, even though the event took place two millennia ago!

Now that we are becoming somewhat more comfortable with the size of the Universe, don't. There are some credible scientific theories that support the notion that our incomprehensible Universe may be only one of *many* such Universes.

Andrei Linde of Stanford University has incorporated current understanding of quantum physics into a new cosmological model that envisions a vast Cosmos, much larger than our Universe. We imagine our Universe to be unique, but Linde believes it is only one of an immense number...perhaps an infinite number...of equally valid, equally independent, equally isolated universes. Our Universe may be just "one island in the cosmic archipelago," in the words of Martin Rees.

I know. Attempting to unravel the intricacies of *this* Universe is challenging enough. I'm only trying to lay the groundwork for the heart of this manifest; i.e., that the Universe (or universes) is only a part of a larger, grander plan. And the process of unraveling this plan is the most exciting part of living. Try not to become comfortable with certainty.

Dr. Hans Holzer writes:

"For we must never forget that we are neither at the pinnacle of scientific discovery, nor at the end of the road leading toward a better understanding of the universe. For all we know, we may be at the very beginning, certainly no further along the way than the middle, at best. It is one of the fallacies of modern science to think of itself as having reached great heights beyond which lies little that is new. The opposite is true and, in the course of future discoveries, many previously held ideas concerning the nature of the universe will have to fall by the wayside."

Holzer's insight is reflected throughout this book. Along our path, wherever it leads us, we'll go much farther when we jettison this one common mistake...we think we already know the nature of reality. We'll learn a lot more if we stop pretending to have a superior vantage point or a final answer. Perhaps the best place to start is with the understanding that we really don't know how the Universe works.

Everyday reality is comfortable. It affords a protection we feel we cannot do without.

So, in the face of such overpowering galactic numbers depicting the size of the Universe, what is the likelihood that an *inhabited* planet, Earth, accompanying one ordinary star, our Sun, represents the sum total of intelligent life in the Universe? We're it. Why should we, tucked away in a far-flung spiral arm of this Galaxy, be so fortunate?

Let's end this chapter by returning to the chapter's beginning, to that tiny pixel of light, planet Earth, one of thousands appearing in *Voyager 1's* final photograph, the object of Carl Sagan's lamenting.

Astronomer Ann Druyan suggests that we imagine looking at this photo, with its thousands of points of light, and stare at the Earth dot for any length of time "and then try to convince yourself that God created the whole Universe for one of the 10 million or so species of life that inhabit that speck of dust.

Now take it a step further: Imagine that everything was made just for a single shade of that species, or gender, or ethnic or religious subdivision. If this doesn't strike you as unlikely, pick another dot. Imagine *it* to be inhabited by a different form of intelligent life. They, too, cherish the notion of a God who has created everything for their benefit. How seriously do you take *their* claim?"

Chapter 2: But They're So Far Away!

$$N = N^* \; fp \;\; ne \;\; fl \;\; fi \;\; fc \;\; fL$$

Equation gauging the potential number of planets with technologically advanced life in the Milky Way Galaxy ...10,000.

> Dr. Frank Drake
> University of California at
> Santa Cruz

It is illogical and a bit arrogant to believe we are the only beings in God's creation. It is both logical and desirable that "they" exist, since all that God creates gives glory to God the Creator.

> Monsignor Corrado Balducci
> Special Emissary to the
> Holy See

In Chapter 1, we concluded that the Universe is a very big place. In this chapter, we want to talk about the next logical question. Does this big place consist of unfathomable amounts of inorganic matter migrating through vast oceans of empty space, with humans on planet Earth the only existing organic, self-aware beings in the Universe?

We could, of course, fill a small library with the plethora of books written on possible life beyond Earth. And we are not going to attempt to conclusively settle any arguments here. This book is *not* a treatise on UFO's!

Again, I only ask the reader to connect the dots intuitively. Dot #1 was covered in Chapter 1; i.e., we live in an inconceivably immense Universe. Everyone accepts this reality. There is no argument. The purpose of Chapter 1 was to give you a little taste of just how big it is.

This chapter presents Dot #2. If the Universe is as large as previously described, does it make sense to believe that we are the only self-aware beings in it?

About 40 percent of adults in the United States accept the contention that humans are the only intelligent life form in the Universe. This validity is based, in part, on the belief that in the absence of any scientifically verifiable evidence, we must accept our solitary status until proven otherwise.

Five hundred years ago, the astronomer Copernicus was condemned as a heretic for claiming that the Earth wasn't at the center of the Universe, but rather only a small part of it. Now we all chuckle at the thought. Meanwhile, five centuries later, many still believe that we are the *biological* center of the Universe. They refuse to accept that intelligent life exists beyond our planet unless they personally bump into an ET at Wal-Mart! Is this attitude really any different from "assumptions" of 500 years ago?

Dr. Frank Drake is professor of astronomy and astrophysics at the University of California at Santa Cruz. His rather famous, decades-old formula projecting other-world possibilities graces the heading of this chapter. He writes that evidence supports the idea that there are countless systems of living things in the Universe. He states in the December 16, 1993, edition of USA Today that there are "perhaps tens of thousands of civilizations in *our* galaxy, and even more abodes of more primitive life."

Dr. Drake goes on to say that everything we know about the formation and evolution of the solar system, planets and of life on Earth, "says that the whole sequence of events was the result of completely normal and, in fact, inevitable processes. So what happened in our solar system and on Earth should have happened in many, many places."

Astronomer Carl Sagan performed his own calculations on the number of communities in our Milky Way Galaxy that may have attained a technical capability in advance of ours.

His conclusion? "The number of extant civilizations substantially in advance of our own in the galaxy today is perhaps between 50,000 and 1 million," as written in *Intelligent Life in the Universe.*

Harvard psychiatrist John Mack writes in his book *Abduction* about the growing collapse of a worldview that has placed mankind "at the epicenter of intelligence in a cosmos perceived as largely lifeless and meaningless. As we…permit ourselves to surrender the illusion of control and mastery of our world, we might discover our place as one species among many whose special gifts include unusual capacities for caring, rational thought and self-awareness. As we suspend the notion of our preeminent and dominating intelligence, we might open to a universe filled with life-forms different from ourselves to whom we might be connected in ways we do not yet comprehend."

"But they're so far away!"

This is perhaps the most frequent position put forth for the implausibility of extraterrestrial visitation. The position states that any civilization intent on visiting Earth would have to be fast and long-living. A comparatively short jaunt from our closest star neighbor, Proxima Centuri, a distance of 25 trillion miles, would take 300 years at ten million miles an hour, about 250 times faster than our fastest spacecraft travels.

From the same book, Dr. Sagan again offers a pointed insight. He certainly understands that interstellar space flight is far beyond our present technical capabilities. "But there seems to be no fundamental physical objections to preclude, from our own vantage point, the possibility of its development by other civilizations."

Dr. Steven Greer is one of the world's foremost experts on the subject of possible civilizations beyond our solar system. He is a medical doctor who is also director of the Center for the Study of Extraterrestrial Intelligence (CSETI).

Dr. Greer writes in *Extraterrestrial Contact* that it is a commonly held view that, in a Universe containing billions of galaxies, each with billions of star systems, it is highly likely that intelligent life forms have evolved. "However, what is frequently left out of this analysis," he writes, "is the question of *how* such life-forms might utilize laws of physics not currently known to 20th century Earth scientists, how such a utilization may appear to humans, and how we might regard it should we encounter such technologies."

Steven Greer states that "any advanced non-human life capable of interstellar travel will possess technologies which will look like magic to us. They will be using technologies which by-pass linear space-time as we know it. That is, they must drop out of linear time-space reality and actuate communication and travel using technologies...and spectra of reality...way outside of the electromagnetic spectrum."

After 35 years of observing ET phenomenon at various times, Greer is "convinced that through frequency shifts and very high energy physics, these objects and the life forms within them move between linear space-time and other spectra of physical energy and physical reality outside of current detection capabilities. Some have called this inter-dimensional or multi-dimensional shifting." According to Greer, they exceed "the crossing point of light."

What is beyond the crossing point of light? What do you experience when you exceed the speed of light and electrons and even elementary particles? "By definition," Greer says, "any ET civilization that is here has interstellar travel and communications technology. This means they operate on the other side of the light/matter barrier as easy as we use radio signals and fly jets. This is their reality and world."

But how does the physics work? The beauty of the answer goes beyond physics. The answer addresses fundamental tenants of creation itself. The answer touches the heart of this book. It may even allow us to touch the face of God.

Chapter 3: Nonlocal Reality: Touching the Face of God

I have begun to feel that there is a tendency in 20th Century science to forget that there will be a 21st Century science, and indeed a 30th Century science, from which vantage points our knowledge of the universe may appear quite different that it does to us. We suffer, perhaps, from temporal provincialism, a form of arrogance that has always irritated posterity.

Dr. J. Allen Hynek
Northwestern University
astronomer

For any human being in existence to think that there is nothing in the whole world superior to himself would be an insane piece of arrogance.

Chrysippus,
Greek philosopher

The answer to the question of "how" described by Dr. Greer is Dot #3 and brings the mystical down to Earth…sometimes literally! The answer is nonlocal reality.

Discussing nonlocal reality is a challenge, to say the least. It isn't the stuff of dinner table conversation. But I think it's important to provide a taste of its meaning and implications at this juncture in the book. It will help you to understand ideas presented later because, in some respects, nonlocal reality is the glue that holds together the beautiful mosaic of Creation in all its awesome manifestations.

Several of my siblings who reviewed a draft of this chapter in its early stages suggested the chapter should be jettisoned unless I wanted an audience of one. They felt the subject matter, nonlocal reality, was too complicated to comprehend.

I agree.

But I believe that acquiring even an elementary understanding of the concept of nonlocal reality was crucial to glimpsing the true nature of what I'm trying to convey in this book. I'm trying to connect the dots between the size of the Universe and the countless self-aware beings of countless civilizations who live in it, the relationship of the Creator to His numerous created beings and the ability of these beings to tap directly into and experience the magnificent energy that creates and powers the Universe...the Creator's Love.

Nonlocal reality is the foundation of this idea. If I tried to skirt the topic, I'd be shortchanging you. In addition, this book is also written for my son's future children and their children. These children already occupy a special place in my heart. On some level, I already know and love them. I truly believe they will live and prosper in an era when nonlocal reality and other concepts drafted herein are simply taken for granted. I want them to know that their grandfather wasn't afraid to step out of time to suggest alternative realities, and that *they* shouldn't possess this apprehension, either, about subjects in their time that may exist in a different paradigm. (However, in deference to my siblings' suggestion, I extensively edited this chapter with the hope of keeping an audience of at least *two*.)

One person compared this dilemma to a Bob Dylan concert. "One should not expect to understand anything, but hey, that's Bob Dylan up there on stage! The mere fact that there exists a theory that allows us to even talk about something like inter-dimensional travel is simply astounding. Who cares if we understand it?"

So, let's begin.

Although we left Chapter 2 wondering how ET's could travel so far, so quickly (you *were* wondering, weren't you?), the answer to the dilemma goes far beyond Star Trek stuff. It involves nonlocal reality intimately. Nonlocal reality touches every facet of existence. It resides at the foundation of most religious and spiritual traditions, but usually goes by terms such as Being, the Absolute or, perhaps, the Transcendent. It provides a means to personally experience the Creator at His most fundamental level at the point of creation itself. It is the profound ecstatic experience often stumbled across by mystics such as Thomas Aquanis and Teresa of Avila who speak of beatific visions and the direct experience of God...touching the face of God, if you will.

This transcendent field was for many centuries considered only in terms of mysticism. However, the evolution of scientific study in the present generation, especially quantum physics, has ushered Being to the level of scientific scrutiny.

Everything stems from nonlocal reality, the Transcendent, whether we're talking about how space travelers transcend the limits of space-time, how matter manifests or how we can saturate the Divine nature of God into our lives in a manner that spontaneously aligns our actions with the will of God.

Let's look at this nonlocal reality a little closer and try to garner a glimpse of its true relevance to our lives. But it's *only* a glimpse. Quantum theory is a difficult concept to understand. The few insights presented here can do no more than lift a small corner of the veil of mystery.

To begin, the term "nonlocal reality" is about as non-descript as you can get for a term that has such profound significance. Quantum physicists are not generally known for their poetic nomenclature. (It might be easier if we start referring to it as NLR.)

Some physicists have postulated that the Universe came from a quantum "nothing," or pure space-time, without matter or energy.

Dr. Stephen Hawking has suggested in his book *Black Holes and Baby Universes and Other Essays* that the Universe may have sprung into being from nothing, in the form of a particle of space and time resembling an extremely small, slightly irregular, wrinkled sphere in four dimensions.

Dr. Edward Tryon of Hunter College in New York proposed that the entire Universe may have been created as a "vacuum fluctuation," a random quantum leap from the vacuum into a full-fledged Universe!

The Nobel Prize-winning physicist Max Planck shocked the world with his references to the unseen forces of nature. In accepting the Nobel Prize for his study of the atom in the early 20th century, he made a remarkable statement: "As a man who has devoted his whole life to the most clear-headed science, to the study of matter, I can tell you as the result of my research about the atoms this much: 'There is no matter as such!' All matter originates and exists only by virtue of a force which brings the particles of an atom to vibration and holds this most minute solar system of the atom together…We must assume behind this force the existence of a conscious and intelligent mind. This mind is the matrix of all matter."

Dr. Deepak Chopra writes, "In the subatomic world, there are no objects. Only oscillating possibilities. And all these possibilities exist simultaneously."

We aren't required to salute these ideas as fact. However, these testimonies are increasingly altering the very foundations of how we view reality by offering evidence that the foundation of all creation…every elementary particle to every quasar…is a *nonlocal* essence that is present at every point in time and space and matter, and yet isn't *bound* by any point in time or space or matter.

Play that again, Sam?

I understand the paradox. I'm fascinated with the discoveries of quantum physics, but I have a difficult time grasping even its most fundamental tenets. That's because, like most people, I'm used to living in a world where time is sequential, the distance between two points is a straight line, and water always runs down hill.

But like it or not, the laws of physics at the quantum level behave differently. At this level, sequential time is an illusion, space and time are inseparably part of the same dimension, and gravity has little relevance. In the quantum field, light behaves like a wave *and* a particle, particles can "know" what is happening elsewhere, and even a particle's position and speed can't be determined simultaneously. And "particles" are not really a "thing" at all!

There are books available for the layperson interested in learning more about this fascinating and esoteric subject. They're great fun to read if you're willing to barter a complete understanding of the subject in exchange for the magical feeling of wonder derived from discerning that physical existence is only the joyful interplay of clouds of unknowing! It's *better* than a Dylan concert!

Now, back to the show.

First of all, how does this seemingly paradoxical nonlocal essence relate to the physics of interstellar travel…to the crossing point of light?

As we just stated, many physicists believe there is a fundamental form of energy that is absolutely stable. The relative world arises as perturbations of this absolute energy, and all forms of physical energy are manifestations of this absolute state of *unmanifested* energy. This is the source of all matter and energy; Einstein's ever-elusive unified field.

Another attribute of this absolute state is nonlocal reality. Its essential essence is that all that exists is *always* connected and *accessible* through this nonlocal, integrated aspect of existence.

We live in a profoundly interconnected world. The most exciting research in quantum physics today is the investigation of what physicist David Bohm calls quantum-interconnectedness or nonlocal correlations. It has now been demonstrated repeatedly, in laboratories around the world, that quanta of light that are emitted in opposite directions from a source at the speed of light, maintain their connection to one another, and that each little proton is affected by what happens to its twin, many miles away. This surprising coherence between distant entities is called nonlocality. In writing on the philosophical implications of nonlocality, physicist Henry Stapp of the University of California at Berkeley states that this quantum connection could be the "most profound discovery in all of science."

Advanced extraterrestrial civilizations have been able to functionally utilize the effect of this knowledge…that everything is nonlocal. To them, every point in time and space functions as a *window*, or entrance to every *other* point in time and space. A nonlocal interaction links up one location with another without crossing space, and without delay. A nonlocal interaction is, in short, unmediated, unmitigated and immediate. That's why a quick trip across the Galaxy presents no major obstacles to those ET civilizations that have learned how to harness NLR.

To me, this concept not only makes sense from the perspective of quantum physics, but it transcends science to touch the very essence of "how" the Creator creates. I think it's an absolutely *extraordinary* and inspiring concept that the Universe could be integrated in such a fashion that there is absolute integration at every level, although it certainly isn't a universally accepted tenet…yet. The mystics may be correct when they say that one can behold the Universe in a drop of water. Or, as the ancient seers declared in the Vedic Upanishads: "I am That, thou art That, all This is That, That alone is, and there is nothing else but That."

What a *beautiful* paradox!

Now, let's try to draw a connection between NLR and a term previously referenced that is frequently used to reference the source of creation in spiritual literature: Being.

Being is often referred to as the state of eternal unity, the Absolute unmanifested aspect of God. Without undergoing any change in Itself, Being assumes the role of the multiplicity of creation, the diversity of Being. This Absolute state of complete nothingness assumes the role of relativity. But it is nothing but the very nature of Absolute Being…God…appearing in different manifestations. This is why, while the Absolute is eternal in its never-changing status, the relative diversity of creation is eternal in its ever-changing nature.

I think this explanation, believe it or not, resolves the entire enigma of creation! So if you want to stop reading this book now, it's okay. You've just received the answer to what is perhaps the most vexing question to challenge the mind of humankind!

You're still a little confused? It's understandable. Suggesting that everything manifests from nothing is an idea that has usually been assigned to the realm of faith…a mystery best left unsolved. And that's okay. However, if you are still listening for the whispers… listen more closely.

We can't perceive Being with our senses. We can't understand it with our intellect. We are trained to see only the multiplicity and separation of Creation, the stuff of our three- dimensional world. This focus on what is manifested *overshadows* the state of Being. As a result, we think we are separate, including separate from the Creator. It is a perceptual defect that the practices of all religions, in the form of rituals, prayers and meditation, attempt to correct.

Philosopher Timothy Freke writes, "We suffer from an illness of the illusion of separateness. We believe that the world is full of discrete things, when in fact it is all one interconnected whole. We experience ourselves as conscious skin-bags living in a transitory moral life, when in fact we are the eternal mind of the universe."

"The eye with which I perceive God is the same eye with which God perceives me," writes the great Christian mystic, Meister Eckhart.

Let's go back and look at this enigma again and try to connect some dots.

Remember that quantum physics tells us that physical creation emanates from a state of nothingness, the source of NLR. But this "nothingness," according to quantum physics, is the source of everything. It gives rise to everything, yet retains its status as an unmanifested state. This is science talking. Now let's try to translate this scientific jargon into spiritual terms in order to see more clearly the eclectic connection between these two seemingly disparate worlds.

Start by substituting the term NLR with Being, and the previous paragraph reads the same, as follows: Being (nothingness), the Absolute unmanifested aspect of God (the quantum source of everything), without undergoing any change in Itself (retains its quantum status as an unmanifested state), assumes the role of the multiplicity of creation (gives rise to everything). Do you see this incredible connection? Quantum physics and spirituality seem to be quickly converging to a common reference point where we may eventually perceive little difference between NLR and Absolute Being.

Of course, this supposition does not address the *source* of creation's spark...the Creator. We'll look at this question of source and the reason for the Creator's desire to create in later chapters.

We have been lead to believe, and it is certainly our own experience, that we are separate from the Creator. We're not, *but it's impossible to understand with the intellect alone.* Once we reach a level of consciousness or awareness, via a perfected nervous system, which allows us to bridge experientially the gap, we realize in no uncertain terms that the gap or separation never existed. Or, as the Bhagavad Gita exclaims, it is "maya," or illusion.

Now, let's take NLR and Being a step further and suggest that mind, that difficult-to-define abstraction usually associated with some component of our brain, *also* displays the same characteristics of NLR and Being.

Just like nonlocal reality, the true nature of *mind* is that it is indivisible and present at every point in time and space...but isn't bound or limited by any aspect of space or time. This means that both distant points in space and time can be assessed through this faculty. In fact, NLR, Being and mind are all essentially one and the same.

I think this knowledge will form the basis of the next major step in scientific exploration...the study of the relationship between *consciousness* and nonlocal reality.

But that's enough for now. You might want to close the book and ponder on what has just been proposed. And when you're ready, proceed to Chapter 4 and we'll discuss this idea that mind is nonlocal and what it means in terms of consciousness.

Chapter 4: Eternal Mind of the Universe

I've lived on the lip of insanity,
Wanting to know reasons.
Knocking on the door,
The door opens.
I've been knocking from the inside.

Author Unknown

When we left Chapter 3, we stated that the true nature of mind itself is a nonlocal reality, omnipresent, and not bound by space or time. As a nonlocal reality, space and time does not define mind or limit it. In this sense, the total number of minds in the Universe is...one.

"One?"

There is only one mind. There is one awakeness, one light of consciousness shining throughout the Universe and through every individual. In this sense, the individuality of a human or an extraterrestrial life form is a window or opening through which the unbounded mind is shining. The fact that we identify this awakeness with our ego, or our thoughts, or our perceptions is actually an illusion.

As we stated previously, the purpose of religion is to translate this idea of mind into experience. With the exception of a handful of mystics, sages, and glimpses by others immersed in a transcendent state, the experience of a singular or nonlocal mind is only a concept. We may sense its truth, but it's usually a stretch. As we just said, this is because we identify our 'local' mind with our ego, or our thoughts, or our perceptions. This is the illusion.

The actual nature of mind, regardless of how we may understand or perceive it, is beyond space, beyond time and is omnipresent and eternal. This is the fundamental aspect of the existence of every intelligent life form.

By becoming aware of the depths of this silent consciousness, we can awaken to the nonlocal or unbounded aspect of *ourselves*. Mind is at all times in that state, even though we are awake, at sleep, or dreaming. Mind, therefore, is in its essential nature, a singularity, and is not a divisible reality. There are not pieces of mind functioning in different individuals. Pure consciousness is the aspect of every self-aware, intelligent life form, a gateway to the nonlocal Universe. By recognizing the nonlocal nature of mind, and by *experiencing* that state, mind in its pure, silent state, we can actually perceive *anything, anywhere*, at *any point in time or space*.

Have I lost my audience of two?

Let me give you an example that many of us can relate to.

Most of us have had the experience of a precognitive dream about a future event. Not necessarily a history-making event. It could be as simple as the pending visit of your mother-in-law. (I'll resist the time-honored maxim of referring to such a dream as a nightmare.) These dreams take place because we are accessing mind, and since mind in its pure form is not bound by space or time, we can perceive an event in the future from within the present state of time. Because mind is really independent of space or time, it can *access* any point in space or time. This is a genuinely nonlocal event in time that the mind violates the barrier between the present and the future.

Understanding this basic reality of awakeness of mind enables us to begin to experience this state, and then to apply that experience to access nonlocal mind and therefore any point in space or time, or perceiving an event taking place in another part of town, somewhere else on Earth, or even another part of the Galaxy. Moreover, this can take place at any *point* on the spectrum of time.

The important thing to remember is that experience of mind is continual. We are all awake. Usually, and unfortunately, we are only awake to what we are aware of...the *sounds* of my son's boom box...my *thoughts* about what I'd like to do with it... *feeling* the headache it gives me. It takes practice to become aware of awareness itself. As we'll learn later, the tools to experience this awareness consistently lay at the roots of all major religious and spiritual traditions. It is not an intrinsically difficult thing to learn. Trust me here. This experience is such an intimate part of being a conscious, awakened human, but we don't see it. It is almost *too* close. This state has been called by some traditions cosmic consciousness...individual awareness of the universal, silent mind, even though constantly and simultaneously engaged in everyday activities. It is a constant presence.

Of course, extraterrestrial life forms are intelligent life forms that are conscious, awake, just as we are. Remember that the total number of minds is only one. Therefore, the light of awakeness is also shining through, and illuminating, every extraterrestrial life form.

Beyond the question of intelligent life forms, human and extraterrestrial, it is also true that matter itself is awake, that space is awake. There is a nonlocal aspect of matter, of space, as we discussed in the pervious chapter. And it is awake even as we are awake. Every cell in our body is awake, has its own consciousness. This is also true of every atom, every rock...the entire Universe is conscious. So when we look at the stars, see them as awake even as we are awake. It is all consciousness in its most fundamental aspect.

With respect to the discussion of extraterrestrial life forms, it is especially significant that their evolution technologically has assisted them with their ability to interface with consciousness or mind. By virtue of being technologically advanced by perhaps thousands of years, they can communicate and move beyond the barrier of light.

From a research point of view, this means that these space craft and their occupants who have been visiting this sector of the Milky Way Galaxy are able to interact with mind and thought as easily as we use the telephone and speak over radio waves.

Divinity and Nonlocal Mind

The mind is not in the brain, though it may work through it. Where is the mind? In *God and the New Physics*, physicist Paul Davies discusses the error of regarding certain concepts as things requiring a location and made of some sort of stuff. "What stuff is the mind and soul made of?" he asks. "The question is as meaningless as asking what stuff citizenship or Wednesdays are made of. To talk of the mind or soul as being in a place is as misconceived as trying to locate the number seven or Beethoven's Fifth Symphony. Such concepts are not in space at all."

Thus, if the mind, human consciousness, does exist beyond the body, can we "manipulate" this consciousness to enhance mankind's evolution? Without a doubt. We'll look at the tremendous possibilities associated with uplifting the collective consciousness of mankind in the next chapter on the Maharishi Effect. But first I want to address this nonlocal field from another interesting perspective.

Ingenious attempts to assess objectively the effectiveness of "manipulating" this nonlocal field via various ways of praying have been pursued for more than a decade by a unique organization called Spindrift.

A central assumption made by the Spindrift researchers is that all humans have "divine attributes, a qualitative oneness with God." It assumes the existence of a nonlocal quality of human consciousness; consciousness, like the Divine, being infinite in space and time and that is ultimately One.

The first questions asked by the Spindrift researchers are fundamental. Is spiritual healing real, does prayer work, is there an effect that can be measured, is the effect reproducible? One of the simplest ways of answering these questions is to test the interaction of a healer with a simple biological system such as sprouting seeds. If the healer prays for one batch of germinating seeds and not another, is there a difference in the rate of germination?

I'm not going into details on the multiple types of experiments done to text their theories. It is fascinating reading if you care to research the material, especially Dr. Larry Dorsey's *Recovering The Soul: A Scientific and Spiritual Search*. But the end result of their numerous experiments indicated repeatedly with many practitioners that the effect of thought on a variety of living organisms under an assortment of conditions outside the human body was significant, quantifiable and reproducible, and that the effects of human consciousness are not confined to the brain and body.

Similarly, in a rigidly controlled scientific study done on the effect of prayer on humans, cardiologist Randolph Byrd of San Francisco General Hospital conducted a study of 393 patients admitted to the coronary care unit. Roughly half the patients were prayed for by home prayer groups, the other half were not remembered in prayer. The study followed a rigid design, meaning that it was a randomized, prospective, double blind experiment in which neither the patients, doctors or nurses knew which group the patients were in.

Prayer group participants were not told how to pray for their patients, and each participant was assigned between five and seven patients,

The results were striking. The prayed-for patients were five times less likely than the other to require antibiotics, three times less likely to develop pulmonary edema, none required endotracheal intubation versus 12 in the other group, and fewer prayed-for patients died.

The Spindrift and Byrd experiments provide an intriguing insight into the unique connection between the transfer of intentions between subject and object. The ability to use mind, regardless of how you want to define it, to influence the growth of bean sprouts or to heal coronary patients is more than noteworthy. The experiments give credence to the existence of a field...a connection...between subject and object that defies explanation at this point in our scientific evolution. But it exists.

I'd like to take this example of nonlocality and stretch it to encompass a much larger field; the intimate connection between humanity and Divinity postulated by the Spindrift group.

The typical geometry envisioned by most of us when we petition God for His intervention looks like an ordinary triangle. God, of course, sits at the apex. At another angle, the petitioner directs her petition upwards towards God and presents the supplication on behalf of the object located at the third angle... "Dear God, please make grandma well." According to this diagram, prayer is directed upwards along the plain to God, Who ponders the merits of the request and, if deemed meritorious, directs His Grace down the opposite plain to the intended receiver...grandma. (Or reversing the direction back down the *same* plain if our intention is self-directed.) This is the basic prayer scenario taught to all of us from childhood.

However, should the Spindrift and Byrd experiments cause us to pause and consider an alternative to this triad?

Genesis 1:27 says we are made in the image and likeness of God. Isaiah 41:23 proclaims "Ye are Gods." John 14:12 gives us Christ's response to a question concerning His miracles... "And greater works than these shall he do," Christ says. Theologians speak of our Divinity as sparks from the Divine Flame. Most religious traditions speak of this supreme connection, although they tend to ignore its significance by punctuating their dogma from their pulpits with reminders that we are sinful, fallen creatures whose only hope of salvation is through God's generosity. The net result of these back-to-dust preachments from the religious communities has been a near-total disenchantment of the world and all in it, including ourselves...a vulgarization of creation in which any sense of sacredness has been sacrificed.

Be that as it may, let's assume that our Divinity exists and is alive and well. Is our triangular connection with God correct? Does a path really exist between humans and God? Or is this path merely the illusion of separation from the Creator? If we truly share His Divinity, is any intention made "to God" really a petition made from *us* as a Spark of Divinity directly to the intended receiver? If true, then perhaps there is no Divine intercession in the usual sense of the word because in reality we are not separate from the Creator…our intention *is* a Divine intention. So, whether our intention is sprout-directed or a more consequential purpose, the process may be the same.

Aldous Huxley writes that "Our awakening to our Divine nature releases us from the bondage of sequential time where we perceive ourselves on a path 'going to God' through time, hoping to be rescued by the benevolent act of God. Our awakening allows us to wake up to the fact that, now and always, the soul and the Godhead are one and the same.

This is where the concept of nonlocal mind, difficult as it may be to comprehend, helps to clarify this phenomenon. Nonlocal mind by definition precludes separation from anything. It is omnipresent. It's sitting in a hot tub with clothes on; the water permeates every thread. *We* are soaked with nonlocality.

We have been saturated with another kind of reality since birth. Our culture, our religious institutions, constantly reinforces the belief in our separation from God. Christianity dates the separation back to Adam and Eve. Life therefore becomes a constant struggle to reconnect with the Creator, and for most people this is perceived as an impossible task.

It is perceived as an impossible task due to our inability to uncover our Divine nature. But an Awakening cannot occur on the level of the intellect, as testified to by Thomas

Aquanis in this book's Introduction where he states that his mystical vision affected him so profoundly that "I cannot go on. All that I have written seems to me like so much straw compared to what I have seen and what has been revealed to me."

George Jaidar writes in *The Soul: An Owners Manual*, that we should consider ourselves to be *heirs* of God. That we don't have to earn God's love, but simply make a claim to it; it's our inheritance. "What you are heir to is really quite inexpressible, except to say you can discover who you really are…" Also included in his concept of heir is that we "share the qualities or characteristics of God or the Cosmos. But you can discover these only in action. With words, all you can do is point to it."

Thus far I have only been using words to point to it. But you'll read later that this awaking to our inner Divinity almost always involves using a specific technique to make a connection with the field of Being that underlies and supports existence. Infusing Being via our nervous system into our lives uncovers and exposes the Divinity that has always been there…that we received as our birthright. This is true God realization. That is why the Upanishads declare "I am That, thou art That, and all this is That."

The specific technique I recommend in Chapter 7 is Transcendental Meditation ™. I have over 30 years of experience with the technique and the tradition. But I'm often asked if TM is the only way to awaken our Divinity? (Ok, most people don't ask the question *quite* like that.) And the answer is no, of course not. The experiences of the mystics alone provide extensive evidence of other doors. (See Chapter 12.) But as I state in Chapter 7, "I not aware of any other modality focused on altering consciousness that exceeds TM's systematic, effortless nature, supported by literally hundreds of physiological, psychological and societal studies verifying its impact." And for me, one of TM's most salient features is its roots…the ancient Vedas, where the fundamental knowledge was originally cognized directly from the field of Perfect Being by enlightened sages. There is absolutely no doubt in my mind that the TM Program represents the very highest knowledge available to mankind at this time in our history.

I realize that this thesis of humanity's Divinity is blasphemous to some. I can appreciate the consternation many will feel. The idea that humanity and Divinity are a singularity is a difficult bridge to cross. Some will refer to it as pantheism, a term that refers to a belief in a connection between all life forms that diffuses Divinity with the acceptance of the existence of the One Mind idea.

But I'm fascinated by the writings of various saints and sages who express their mystical experiences in terms that only reinforce this belief. Saint Catherine of Genoa described her sense of oneness with the Almighty in explicit, almost shocking terms: "My Me is God, nor do I recognize any other Me except my God himself." The 14th century mystic Meister Eckhart wrote "The knower and the known are one. Simple people imagine that they should see God, as if He stood there and they here. This is not so. God and I, we are one in knowledge." Many more examples appear in Chapter 12, Saints & Mysticism.

These individuals experience a mystical sense of oneness and unity with all there is, what Carl Jung called "the transcendent at-one-ment" that places one in contact with the One Mind. But ultimately this universal Mind and the single mind are one and the same. "Does this mean," writes Jung, "that the Mind is 'nothing but' our mind? Or that our mind is the Mind? Assuredly it is the latter…there is no hubris in this; on the contrary, it is a perfectly accepted truth [in the East], whereas with us [in the West] it would amount to saying 'I am God.'" But although it may seem blasphemous to the Westerner to acknowledge such a thing, this realization, Jung stated, was nonetheless an "incontestable 'mystical' experience" present in all religious traditions, East and West.

And almost to a person, saints and sages lament over their inability to find adequate words to fully explain their beatific experiences. The experiences are beyond language. And some lament over the conflict created between the dogma associated with their religion and their experiential reality engendered by the mystical experience.

Why are we not more aware of these types of experiences? Why are they not more common? Philosopher William Irwin Thompson suggests the reason is that we are suffering a kind of collective hypnosis, a cultural trance that prevents us from seeing things the way they actually are. "We are like flies crawling across the ceiling of the Sistine Chapel," he states. "We cannot see what angels and gods lay underneath the threshold of our perceptions." We lack an awakening process.

We all have a desire, especially the author, to take concepts, beliefs and ideas and categorize them according to some logical format and place them into an orderly, comprehensible package. But the nature of the concepts we're discussing here defy understanding and easy categorization from the level of ordinary consciousness. And as the level of our awareness grows as our consciousness expands, what we understand as truth at one level will only morph at a higher level. Each level of increased awareness will encompass the level before it, but new revelations will only bring us closer to the realization that our perceived separation from the Creator is an illusion. The Vedas proclaim that "knowledge is structured in consciousness." Listen for the whisper.

I realize that this entire discussion of nonlocal reality stretches the boundaries of credibility. During the course of writing this discourse on NLR, I've re-read these paragraphs many, many times, tweaking them in an attempt to make the subject matter easier to understand, while trying not to sacrifice the incredible significance of the subject. And each time I re-read the material, the profundity of the implications of these ideas seems to delve deeper and deeper into my consciousness, continually being validated at a fundamental level of my being.

I'm certainly not the only human impacted to such a profound degree. Many people are experiencing similar awakenings. It seems as if a new paradigm is now forming. These discoveries in quantum field theory certainly defy standard conceptions of how Creation works. We are constantly reassessing the very principals that have traditionally guided scientific research.

This search is opening up science to a paradigm that can finally integrate the realm of Spirit with that of the physical. It is spurring new research on the origins of Creation. It seems that events are establishing the foundation of a grand transformation in society.

We've just briefly examined three crucial pieces of the puzzle that are increasingly seen as having the same common ancestry: nonlocal reality, Being and mind. I think the synchronicity of these three realms will play a significant role in leading mankind to a most *extraordinary* destiny. In the next chapter, we'll begin to witness the practical application of this knowledge in a manner that will help foster the creation of this special destiny.

Chapter 5: The Maharishi Effect

> Darkness cannot drive out darkness; only light
> can do that. Hate cannot drive out hate; only love
> can do that. Hate multiplies hate, violence
> multiplies violence, and toughness multiplies
> toughness in a descending spiral of destruction.
> The chain reaction of evil...hate begetting hate,
> wars producing more wars...must be broken, or
> we shall be plunged into the darkness of
> annihilation.
>
> Martin Luther King

In the last chapter, we stated that the idea of the existence of a nonlocal reality, of a one-mind universe, "stretches the boundaries of credibility."

In this chapter, I'd like to stretch the boundaries a little further.

Using the idea of one-mind as a foundation, I want to suggest that if indeed there is only one mind, then each of us is constantly *contributing* to the constitution of this one-mind.

It only makes sense. With only one mind, each of us contributes our thoughts to the collective soup that constitutes mind. It completely shatters the old paradigm that each of us functions as an island within the sea of humanity. Our collective thoughts and the subsequent deeds emanating from these thoughts function more like a cosmic sponge...an infinite number of canals, constantly connecting and processing the collective thoughts and deeds of its cosmic citizens.

This is not a new idea. There are numerous references in literature to this concept.

For example, in a paper published in 1898, William James suggested "there exists a continuum of consciousness uniting individual minds that could be directly experienced if the psychophysical threshold of perception were sufficiently lowered through refinement in the functioning nervous system." James's paper was a modern reference to a field of consciousness, a level of universal mind, which touches each and every life.

In the words of their day, ancient teachings suggest a similar field of consciousness. The Vedic traditions, for example, speak of a unified field of "pure consciousness" that permeates all of creation. In such traditions, our experience of thought and perception are viewed as *disturbances*, interruptions in an otherwise motionless field. At the same time, it is through our path of mastering perception and thought that we may find the unifying consciousness as individuals or as a group.

This unified field of consciousness is a field of infinite possibilities, and when you cause a slight perturbation in that field, it ripples across the cosmos, much as a stone dropped into a pond produces ripples that flow to its perimeter. At the quantum level, matter has no well-defined edges…it is a wiggle in the unified field. And when there is a clear, collective intent, changes are profound.

In the previous chapter, we talked about the "profundity of the implications of these ideas." But just what *are* the implications?

The implications of this tenet are vast and, at the same time, tremendously relevant. In its broadest sense, our role within a unified field awareness means that there can be no isolated actions, no "them" and "us." No longer can we view the conditions of our world as "their problems" and "our problems." In a field of unified consciousness, each choice that we make and every act we perform in each moment of each day must affect every other person in this world, in this

Universe. Some actions produce a greater effect and some a lesser one. Still, the effect is there.

If each of us is truly connected to each other and to society as a whole, doesn't this connection provide us with unique opportunities to "feed" the collective in a manner that contributes to the upliftment and enlightenment of the whole? Doesn't it also imply a special *responsibility* on our part to think and act in a manner that enhances the whole, now that we realize that we're not individual cosmic islands?

We live in a world of collective consent. The conditions of war and suffering on a large-scale mirror the elements that makes such conditions possible on a small scale. Sometimes consciously, sometimes not, we consent to expressions of our group-will in ways that we may never suspect. On levels that we may not even be aware of, our thoughts, attitudes, and actions toward one another each day contribute to the collective beliefs that 'agree' to the wars and suffering of the world.

"There is no way we can separate ourselves from nature, because we *are* nature," says Deepak Chopra, M.D. "And our brains, our nervous systems, are recycled dust from the stars, and so turbulence in our consciousness naturally reflects the turbulence in the environment, because the environment is not the environment, it's our extended body. If our physical body trembles, then our extended body also trembles. Our bodies, our minds, are inseparably a part of the pattern of intelligence, energy, and information that permeates the cosmos."

For example, the creation of a wartime mentality of expecting and preparing for conflict in our international world can *happen only if we allow for such conflict in our personal lives.* As we live individual episodes of "defending ourselves" in romance and personal relationships, "outsmarting" others in our schools and "out-strategizing" co-workers and competitors, quantum physics reminds us that these individual expressions of our lives pave the way for similar expressions, amplified by many orders of magnitude, in another time and place. To know peace in our world, we must become peace in our lives.

I began writing this chapter in early September 2001. On September 11, the United States was severally impacted by the World Trade Center and Pentagon bombings, as well as the crash of the terrorist-hijacked Flight 93 in western Pennsylvania, just a few miles from my home. The sounds of saber rattling are everywhere.

What do we do? It is abundantly clear that conventional strategies of defense provide no effective defense against terrorism. Clearly, a new approach is required...one that targets the underlying causes of fanatical, violent behavior. Enter here our discussion of the unified field of awareness and collective consciousness.

For the long term, education must expand comprehension, and it must develop the brain fully. It should incorporate the discovery of the unified field, which establishes the ultimate unity of life and of humanity. This knowledge can be effectively conveyed even at primary levels of education. Research shows that the assimilation of such knowledge, together with its associated balanced brain development, virtually precludes narrowly self-centered, violent and destructive behavior. Highly successful examples of this "unified field" based education can be found throughout the world.

But it may take years to modernize education and 'enlighten' the world. In the meantime, we must halt terrorism now. And we can, according to research published in leading scientific journals. These studies add to a growing body of evidence suggesting that large groups of people practicing stress-reducing meditation techniques have a predictable and measurable effect on the quality of life based on the *field effect* of the group meditation. These statistically significant studies have documented changes in daily life, such as a reduction in crime, reduced traffic accidents and fewer hospital admissions. ('Statistically significant' means that the results cannot be easily attributed to any other cause.)

This is where the application of such studies becomes crucial in global efforts to bring peace to our world. If we view conflict, aggression and war in our outer world as indicators of stress in our collective-consciousness, then relieving collective stress should relieve global tensions. In the words of Maharishi Mahesh Yogi, founder of Transcendental Meditation ™, "All occurrences of violence, negativity, conflict crisis, or problems in any society are just the expression of the growth of stress in collective consciousness. When the level of stress becomes sufficiently great, it bursts out into large-scale violence, war and civil uprising necessitating military action." The beauty of the field effect is that *when stress is relieved within a group, the effects are registered beyond the immediate group,* even into a larger area. This is the thinking that led to studies of mass meditation during the Israeli-Lebanese War in the early 1980's.

In September 1983, studies conducted by David Orme-Johnson in Jerusalem explored the relationship between meditation and violence. Applying new technologies to test ancient theory, individuals trained in the techniques of the TM-Sidhi Program were placed in strategic locations within Jerusalem during the conflict with Lebanon. The purpose of the study was to determine if the wave of pure consciousness generated by group practitioners would be reflected as less violence and aggression on a regional basis.

The 1983 studies followed earlier experiments indicating that as little as one percent of a mass population practicing unified forms of meditation was enough to reduce crime rates, accidents and suicides. Studies conducted in 1972 showed that 24 U.S. cities, each with populations over 10,000, experienced a statistically measurable reduction in crime when as few as one percent (100 people for every

10,000) of the population practiced TM. This became known as the "Maharishi Effect."

In the Israeli study, to determine how TM would influence the general population, the quality of life was defined by a statistical index based on the number of fires, traffic accidents, occurrences of crime, fluctuations in the stock market and the general mood of the nation. At the peak of the experiments, 234 participants meditated in the study, a small fraction of the population of greater Jerusalem. The results of the study showed a direct relationship between the number of participants and the decrease of activity in the various categories of quality of life. When the number of participants was high, the index of the various categories declined. Crimes, fires and accidents increased as the number of people meditating was reduced.

These studies demonstrated a high correlation between the number of people practicing the more advanced TM-Sidhi Program and the quality of life in the region. (See note at the end of this chapter defining the TM-Sidhi Program.) Similar studies conducted in major population centers of the United States, India and the Philippines found similar correlations. Data from these cities between 1984 and 1985 verified decreases in crime rates "that could not have been due to trends or cycles of crime or to changes in police policies or procedures."

Social Indicators Research (1999) reported the results of a $6 million project involving 4,000 participants in a TM-Sidhi course during the summer of 1993 in Washington, D.C. Violent crime dropped more than *23 percent* below the level predicted.

For centuries, sages have suggested that only a very small percentage of humanity, working together in a unified effort, could shift the consciousness of the entire world. Just a few individuals can plant the seeds of great possibilities. The studies of the impact of the TM-Sidhi Program just referenced indicate that the impact is generated when the number of people participating in the Program was greater than *the square root of one percent of the population*. In a city of one million people, for example, this value represents only one hundred individuals!

On a global scale, this value offers the potential of powerful results. The square root of one percent of the Earth's population is about 8,000 people. This number represents only the minimum required for the effects to begin. The greater the number participating, the greater the acceleration of the effect.

In *1986*, just before Maharishi assembled the first group of 8,000 Vedic Pandits in India practicing the TM/Sidhi Program, Maharishi made an auspicious comment to all those who were gathered in his garden at Maharishi Nagar. He said that the impact of the group coherence of these 8,000 "soon would be reflected in the dissolution of the Iran and Iraq war, the U.S. and Russia will shake hands and the Berlin wall will fall." His comments were subsequently published in *Maharishi's Plan for World Peace*. Of course, we now know that his comments were propitious.

I attended a TM-Sidhi course in Fairfield, Iowa where these early studies were extensively reviewed. Dr. Larry Domash, a physics professor at Maharishi International University at the time, related to us his conversation with an expert in the social sciences from another university on the significance of the studies. Dr. Domash stated that the expert could not refute either the scientific design of the studies or the statistical significance of the results. However, the social scientist still would not accept the data from the studies because, as he stated to Dr. Domash, he was "not yet prepared to accept the incredible implications of the results."

Coherent light, such as light from an incandescent light bulb, is composed of many frequencies of light energy. It is effective, but not nearly as powerful as a single frequency of light emanating from a light source...like a laser beam. The situation with group work is analogous. When the energy field of the group becomes coherent, it becomes intensified, just as a laser light does. As Dr. William Tiller of Stanford University suggests on the basis of his research work, the intensity of the coherent group-energy field is not the sum of the number of group members but is, instead, the square of the number of people in the group. Thus, the power of a group of 200 people whose energies are coherent would not have a numerical value of 200 but of 40,000 according to Dr. Tiller. The induction potential of a group field can be very powerful.

The "incredible implications" statement made to Dr. Domash and the group-energy work of Dr. Tiller points to the validity of the connectedness of all humanity and the ripple effect of our thoughts and deeds on this human mosaic. There has never been a better time for a new approach...an approach with a demonstrated ability to prevent social violence and stop terrorism. The TM-Sidhi Program is a concrete and measurable force. When we're faced with the frustration of "what can we do" in the face of personal and societal problems, to meditate is to "do" something. The solutions of the past are failing us in the present. Meditation is the act of redefining the foundation of hate, violence and war. The "doing" simply occurs in a form very different from our idea of doing in the past; a *very* significant and powerful difference.

John Heglin, Ph.D., Harvard-trained quantum physicist and the Natural Law Party's 2000 U.S. presidential candidate, stated that "These technologies of consciousness diffuse social stress and negativity and generate positive waves of harmony and unity in the collective consciousness of the world. They access and stimulate the most powerful level of mind and matter, identified by modern science as the Unified Field, the fundamental level of nature's intelligence that connects us all. We now have available a technology of peace, a truly defensive technology that attacks the problems of violence and negativity at their source. Research shows this works."

Over 40 sociological studies have utilized the most advanced research designs and statistical methodologies to evaluate the effect of large coherence-creating groups on standard sociological measures of the quality of life in cities, nations and the world. These studies have rigorously demonstrated the power of the Maharishi Effect to a degree that is unparalleled in the sociological sciences. The Maharishi Effect in itself proves the existence of the unified field of natural law and our ability to operate from this level.

At the beginning of this 21st century, we are at an important threshold. The survival of our species may actually depend upon our ability to merge our inner and outer sciences. As we redefine the roles of political affiliations, military alliances and the boundaries of nations, the power of consciousness-based solutions cannot be discounted. The implications of applying the "technology" of meditation on a global scale are immense.

The profundity of the Maharishi Effect cannot be overstated. Since time immemorial, mankind has been trying to solve problems on the level of the problem. Now we are just beginning to understand and appreciate the implications of collective consciousness. I have little doubt that future generations will accept this reality without question. However, we have to wait until the present collective consciousness of humanity reaches a point where a phase transition in awareness is triggered to bring this incredible reality fully into the light of day.

Whether we refer to ancient texts or quantum physics, we are slowly beginning to understand that there is only one of us here in our world. As we alleviate the pain of others, we alleviate our pain as well. As we love others, we love ourselves. Each man, woman, and child of this world has the power to create a new possibility, to change the thinking that allows suffering.

Certainly, we all desire to alleviate the pain of others, to love others unconditionally. Haven't all religions had this laudable intention as the foundation of their institutions? Then why has this goal been so difficult to experience, despite the existence of our ancient texts providing us with a course of direction?

The answer again brings us back again to the unified field or Being. What is required is the ability to effortlessly establish Being as the foundation of our thoughts, which always precede our actions. Performing actions based on thoughts experienced at the source of Being will guarantee the performance of spontaneous right action in our lives. And spontaneous right action, based on Natural Law emanating from Being, will always reflect the intent of the Creator because the Creator *is* Being!

* * * * * *

TM-Sidhi Program: The sidhis are based on an ancient formula involving the manifestation of thoughts, or sutras, projected from transcendental consciousness, the unified field of natural law. It is a field of all possibilities. Thus, a thought or sutra introduced at this subtle level is easily manifested on the surface level of life. Any intention projected from the unified field of natural law commands the infinite organizing power of natural law for its immediate fulfillment. Every one of us has the ability, through the TM Sidhi Program, to gain the ability to function from this simplest form of our own awareness and can develop mastery over natural law.

Chapter 6: Nobody's Perfect?

> Do everything you can to save this planet, but don't let this planet's death make you waiver for one instant from the glory of your origin. You will only be able to save the planet when you reflect the glory of your origin in every action, in every moment.
>
> Mother Teresa

The prior chapter provides us with insights into how the TM Sidhi Program can naturally create behavior patterns that reflect spontaneous right action. It's a magnificent yet simple process. It is only revolutionary in the sense that it contradicts centuries of established belief...beliefs so instilled in humankind's psyche that we are tempted to dismiss it as some New Age quackery.

However, as discussed in the previous chapter, statistically significant studies have already demonstrated the validity of the impact of *collective* consciousness...the Maharishi Effect. By employing the TM-Sidhi Program to generate ripples from the unified field of consciousness, it reverberates throughout existence, causing profound changes.

Therefore, if the Maharishi Effect is valid in terms of its collective impact on society, wouldn't it make sense that its *primary* impact would occur at the level of *individual* consciousness? In fact, this is exactly what occurs.

By effortlessly establishing Being as the foundation of our thoughts...and thoughts always precede action...we perform action based on thoughts expressed at the source of Being. It increasingly ensures the performance of right action in our lives...spontaneously.

But doesn't religion provide us with the ability to perform right action? To a degree.

But the purpose of religion isn't solely to distinguish between right and wrong. To fulfill its purpose, religion should elevate us to a state of life where we will choose only that which is right and will by *nature* avoid what is wrong. The true spirit of religion is lacking if it only lays down what is right and wrong and creates fear of punishment and hell and the fear of God in our minds. The purpose of religion should be to take *away* all fear. It shouldn't seek to achieve its purpose by instilling a fear of God.

At its roots, every religion understood this reality explicitly. It belongs to the spirit of every religion. It existed in the early days of every faith, but has since been lost. The principle is still contained in most scriptures. It has only been lost in religious practice.

Unfortunately, our religious teachers seem to have put the cart before the horse. They advise us to behave righteously, teaching that right action will assist us in gaining purity and eventually the realization of God-consciousness. The right approach would be to offer a *direct* way of gaining God consciousness. Established in higher consciousness, we would naturally behave righteously, spontaneously, without constant, conscious reference to a set of commandments.

St. Teresa of Avila never tires of emphasizing in *Interior Castle* that, as one descends (transcends) into successive mansions, virtues are rooted ever more deeply in the personality and practiced with "increasing ease." "Even though one never thinks about virtues," she writes, "they are implanted in a wonderful way."

Any teaching of right action without a means of raising consciousness will always be ineffective. It is much easier to raise our consciousness than to get us to consistently act righteously.

Of course, this discussion of spontaneous right action leads us to an interesting conclusion. If an individual increasingly performs right action based on a consistent regimen of contact with the state of Being, wouldn't that individual eventually reach a state where his or her *every* action would naturally be correct? In other words, a perfect person?

Time out! A perfect person?

"Nobody's perfect." We frequently hear this axiom as testimony to this platitude. Many of us would actually be embarrassed to give credence to such an outrageous idea. This is how far humanity has fallen away from its Divine roots.

Most of us express a belief in some version of the Biblical dictum that we are created in the "image and likeness of God." I often use the notion that we are "Sparks from the Divine Flame." St. Matthew writes in 5:48 of the Bible... "Be ye therefore perfect, even as your Father in Heaven is perfect." We give token acknowledgement to Matthew's declaration, but not many of us really believe it. Religion has done a terrible injustice over the centuries in smothering this beautiful and completely possible reality.

I believe that our search for perfection can really be viewed as a search for something that is already ours. If we were created in the image and likeness of a perfect God, wouldn't we automatically, at some level, inherent His perfection...His Divinity?

I realize that you may find this idea difficult to accept. You may even find it sacrilegious. But, as I wrote in the Introduction, the purpose of this book is to pose questions, some of which may make you uncomfortable. But please continue to listen to the whispers...

Part of the problem stems from the foundation of religion in the West. In the roots of Western religions, God made the world and God and the world are not the same. There is an essential distinction between the Creator and His creation.

The goal of Western religions is not to bring about a sense of identity with the Divine. Their goal is to bring about a relationship between human beings and God, who, they contend, is not the same. In the Western tradition, the Divine is not within us. When we turn within, we are supposed to find a human soul and that soul may or may not be in alignment with its Creator. It tells us that our nature is essentially corrupt and that a great fall took place, whether we designate the fall as Original sin or not. In Western religions, our relationship with God is accomplished through the church...the institution. The church dissociates the person from the Divine principle. This chasm between Divinity and humanity is the root cause of our fear of God.

Let's try something at this point. Take a moment and slowly, silently repeat this phrase three times... "fear of God...fear of God...fear of God." Now listen for the whisper. Do you hear a subtle yet unmistakable whisper coming from deep within your heart that contradicts this phrase? Does the whisper make you feel uncomfortable that the words "fear" and "God" are uttered in the same sentence? It certainly makes *me* uncomfortable. God is not the power of fear. Unfortunately, there are religions whose main platform is the fear of God, and this fear is instilled in the children of God. It is cruel and detrimental to life to spread fear in the name of God.

Now, let's continue this dialogue with the possibility that the whisper is voicing the truth.

First, I think it's important to state clearly that 'God' is the most highly cherished idea in human life for those who understand it. The conception of God is a reality greater than the reality of any conception that the human mind has ever developed.

Second, I've come to believe that God is found in two phases of this reality...as a Supreme Being of absolute, eternal nature, and as a personal God at the pinnacle of creation.

Thus God has two aspects, the personal and the impersonal. They are the two realities of God.

The impersonal aspect of God is formless. It is the Divinity that rests silently at the core of our Being. It is without attributes, because all attributes belong to the relative field of life. But at the same time, It is the source of all relative creation.

The world today has a very vague conception of God. There are those who like to believe in God, those who love God and those who want to realize God. But, even they don't have a clear conception of what God is. God has remained for the most part a fanciful, pleasant thought and a refuge during suffering and misery in life. For the custodians of some religions, God is a magic word to control the understanding and religious destiny of many innocent souls. God, the omnipresent essence of life, is presented as something to fear. As I stated above, God is *not* the power of fear. God is not anything from which fear could emanate.

The other aspect of God is the personal God. God in personal form is the Supreme Being of almighty nature. Our personal God has a form, a specific nature and many attributes, including the ability to command the entire existence of the cosmos. His abilities on every level of life are unlimited.

The key to experiencing the bliss of the personal aspect of God, the God most familiar to our intellect, is through the vehicle of transcendence *to* the level of the impersonal God at the source of creation, the unbounded field of pure Being. To get there, our conscious mind must transcend all the limits of experience in the relative field and enter into a field beyond existence.

However, our actions on the playing field of life are opposed to the essential nature of our inner Divinity at this unbounded field. Divinity is absolute, pure existence. (It's synonymous with the ever-illusive unified field, the quintessential quest of quantum physics.) On the other hand, action is the instrument through which the cycle of life and death is continually kept going. The essential nature of activity is not in conformity with the essential nature of Divinity, which is just to be…pure existence.

No activity can ever reach the state of Divinity. Activity moves continuously through the cycle of life and death. But any process that works to bring activity to an end *will* result in the direct experience of the state of Divinity and will eventually permanently establish this perfected state in the nervous system of the individual. This is the crux of the contention that perfection is not only possible, but is our *birthright*. The attainment of higher states of consciousness has historically been considered rare and difficult. But new research reveals that "enlightenment," the full development of human consciousness, is truly our birthright…a spontaneous by-product of balanced neurophysiological functioning.

Most of us are fully engaged in the relative field of activity. It's very difficult to permeate the value of Divinity into our life because of the overshadowing of activity. This immersion in the field of activity…in the good and the bad…maintains life in the relative field, keeping us out of the realm of Divinity.

An obvious question now arises. How can we avoid the grip of activity and allow the pure existence of Divinity to permeate into the relative field of our existence…to experience the euphoric bliss of God? How can we transcend relativity and literally touch the face of God, our Divinity?

We have been conditioned to believe that there is no way to minimize the force of activity and rising above its influence to attain…to *experience*…the state of Divinity. Thus, a tremendous gulf has evolved over the centuries between spiritual and material values.

However, there are ways to infuse our activity by the Light of Divinity. This is the reason for techniques such as the

TM-Sidhi Program...to allow the mind to literally transcend the relative state of existence and attain the state of pure Being. And, within that state of Divinity, the mind is infused with the value of Divinity because, while in this state, the mind is outside the field of activity, ceases to be individual mind and becomes one with Divinity. Divine Mind.

Of course, this is a life-long process. The transcending process has to be habitual, much like the dying of cloth by repeatedly immersing it into a vat of dye and drying it in the full sun. And for most of us, we're probably looking at more than one lifetime before the full influence of Divinity can completely overshadow relativity to allow the full nature of Divinity to express itself...as perfection. (More than one lifetime? See Chapter 11, Here We Go Again.)

Fortunately, the habitual influence of Divinity begins to be expressed in our lives as a growing tendency to live spontaneously within the laws of nature, including the experience of increasing bliss while in the relative. Eventually, this influence is complete, and the individual reaches a state of enlightenment or perfection.

Historically, monasteries were established to shut out the world of experience, to separate the monk from outside influence...to focus strictly on spiritual advancement. This view reflects a lack of understanding of the true nature of the differences between spirituality and activity, as we just discussed. What was missing was a means to transcend activity. Once we are capable of practicing a technique to regularly infuse the Divine into activity, then our place of residence means little.

It may seem from this discussion that Divinity is an actual place we can locate on Map Quest. However, I've been trying to make the case that Divinity rests at the foundation of all creation. It is not creation itself...it remains unbounded while simultaneously giving rise to creation. The trick is to experience these perturbations or impulses of creation as close to the source of creation as possible and to manifest the purity and intensity of the energy at that pure level into our relative life. Then life...our life...spontaneously reflects the nature of that purity into our individual actions.

William Johnston, SSJ, writes in *The Still Point* that "mystical prayer (meditation) goes deep, and the virtues it implants spring so spontaneously from the inner core of one's being that they are practiced with ease."

Mind originally emanates from this pure field during the course of its "travels" to relative awakening, influenced along the way by a menagerie of increasingly denser thoughts. The filters get clogged. Meditation unclogs the filters to allow the perfection of Divine Intelligence to shine through. This is the skill in action that infuses the power of Divinity into the field of activity through the vehicle of the mind. This glorifies activity at all levels and yet leaves the mind free from the bondage of activity. This freedom of the mind is due to its being full in Divinity. Just as in bright sunlight candlelight loses its significance, so also in the eternal Light of Divinity, the relative joys of life...materialism...lose their grip on the mind. Thus, the mind is freed from the binding influence of activity through the experience of the absolute bliss of Divinity.

Beautiful!

The following indented material provides further insight into this magnificent process, and is taken directly from Maharishi Mahesh Yogi's *Science of Being and the Art of Living*. Maharishi is quoted extensively because his words perfectly express how this process works, and is a key to understanding the basic foundation of this book.

> Although the nature of activity and the nature of Divinity are incompatible, it is possible to glorify activity by the bliss of Divinity. It is possible for us to live in the field of action and yet to live simultaneously a life of freedom in the consciousness of Divinity. It is possible for us to live fully

immersed in worldly activities and yet to live simultaneously in God consciousness, thereby uniting the values of Divinity and relative existence.

Uniting the values of Divinity and relative existence = increased happiness = perfection = enlightenment.

I have no doubt that enlightened, perfect people exist. My experience with 30 years of transcending with Transcendental Meditation confirms the validity of the above discourse and provides a constant beacon of Light leading the way to further evolution. For me, it is not a matter of whether perfection is possible on this plane, but rather when.

But a belief has existed for many generations that the nature of relative existence and the nature of Being are incompatible. (Refer to the previous paragraph in this chapter on the roots of Western religions.) Without an experiential understanding of the nature of Being, religious institutions have perpetuated the notion that we are separate from Being (God). This misunderstanding has created the gulf that has existed for many centuries between spiritual and material values. *This misunderstanding has been the main reason for the growth of suffering, misery, tension and increasing negativity in all areas of life.*

But now is an opportune time to correct this mistake, to realize that through the system of transcendental meditation, it is possible for every mind to go beyond the relative state of experience and attain the state of Being. Having been in that state, the mind is infused with the value of Being. Subsequently, when the mind is drawn out again into the relative field of activity, it realizes that the state of transcendental Being, in its unlimited aspect of absolute bliss, is far better than the relative state of transitional happiness in the field of relativity.

The bliss consciousness of the Transcendent makes an immediate impression upon the nature of the mind. Returning into the relative field where time, space and causation hold everything between narrow boundaries, the mind begins to retain some of this unbounded status. And with repeated practice it becomes more and more familiar with the Transcendent.

The continued practice of transcendental meditation results in such a strong infusion of Being into the nature of the mind that the mind, while continuing to behave and experience in the field of relative existence, begins to live the nature of eternal Being. This has tremendous practical value for the mind engaged in day-to-day activities.

Skill in action requires that activity should first be reduced to nil and from that point action should be started. It can be compared with drawing back an arrow on the bow in order to shoot it ahead. The skill lies in pulling back the arrow on the bow as far as possible until a state of no activity is reached. From that point the arrow is shot without effort by simply releasing the hold. Skill in action is only a matter of pulling back the arrow and releasing it. Then it will shoot ahead naturally with the minimum effort and maximum force.

Likewise, by bringing the activity of the mind to a state of stillness and from that point starting action, the minimum of energy will be required. The action will be performed easily and will yield maximum results. The doer will act while established in eternal freedom of Being and will therefore not be under the binding influence of karma. This is skill in action.

We may thus conclude that, although the nature of karma and the nature of Being are incompatible, it is possible to glorify karma by the bliss of Being. It is possible for man to live in the field of action and yet to live simultaneously a life of eternal freedom in bliss-consciousness of absolute Being. It is possible for a man to act with full interest in the world and yet to live simultaneously in God-consciousness, thereby uniting the values of absolute and relative existence.

To reveal this truth is the ultimate purpose of this book!

It should be stated that while the science of being is complete in its theory, it is essentially a *practical* science in which results depend on the practice of TM. Every one of us can experience this state of Being and create a state of eternal freedom in our lives, while bringing greater success to all fields of activity.

This explanation helps to explain why there is such a significant gulf between the altruistic foundations all of religions and the reality of suffering and disappointment experienced by most of us. A continuing saga of generally unsuccessful attempts to create more perfection in our lives characterizes this reality.

As previously stated, our language constantly spits forth aphorisms that remind us of our shortcomings... "Nobody's perfect." "Without suffering, there would be no compassion." "Man was born into Original sin." And one of my favorites... "There but for the grace of God go I." Mistakes and suffering clearly are seen as accepted facts of life. This is because the foundation of our actions doesn't emanate directly from pure Being. It emerges from the grosser level of creation.

> We find gross things to see with our eyes, gross words or sounds to hear with our ears, gross odors to smell with the nose, varieties of sensations to feel with the sense of touch and varieties of flavors to taste with the tongue. We think, and normally the process of thinking seems to have no connection with these senses of perception. But the process of thinking *does* include one or many of these senses.

Our experience in the field of perception shows that we experience gross and subtle things. We use microscopes to enhance our vision, and amplifiers to improve our hearing. This is the case with all senses of perception. They are only able to experience gross objects. The subtle fields are beyond our ordinary range of experience, even though we know they exist.

But if we could develop our faculty of experience through any of the senses, or develop our ability to experience thought *before* it reaches the conscious level of the mind, and if this ability to experience thought could be so developed that it reached the *source* of thought, then having transcended the source, it would be possible to reach the transcendental state of pure Being. In this way, by progressively experiencing finer states of creation through one of the senses until the finest experience is transcended, the state of Being is reached.

Since Being is by nature transcendental, It does not belong to the range of any of the senses of perception. Only when sensory perception has come to an end can the transcendental field of Being be reached. As long as we experience through the senses, we are in the relative field. Therefore, Being cannot be experienced through any of the senses. This shows that through whichever sense of experience we proceed, we must first reach the ultimate limit of experience through that sense. Then, transcending that, we will reach a state of consciousness in which the experiencer no longer experiences.

Maharishi continues...

The word experiencer implies a relative state; it is a relative word. For the experiencer to exist, there has to be an object of experience. The experiencer and the object of experience are both relative. When we have transcended the experience of the subtlest object, the experiencer is left by himself without an experience, without an object of experience, and without the process of experiencing. When the subject is left without an object of experience, having transcended the subtlest state of the object, he steps out of the process of experiencing and arrives at the state of Being. The mind is then found in the state of Being which is beyond the relative field.

The state of Being is neither a state of objective nor of subjective experience, because both these states belong to the relative field of life. When the subtlest state of an objective experience has been transcended, then the individual's subjectivity merges into the transcendent. This state of consciousness is known as pure existence, the state of absolute Being.

This is how, by bringing the attention to the field of the transcendent, it is possible to contact and experience Being. It cannot be experienced on the level of thinking because, as far as thinking goes, this is still a field of relative existence; the whole field of sensory perception lies within relative existence.

The transcendental state of Being lies beyond all seeing, hearing, touching, smelling and tasting, beyond all thinking and beyond all feeling. This state of unmanifested, absolute, pure consciousness of Being is the ultimate state in life. It is easily experienced through the system of Transcendental Mediation.

Spontaneous Fulfillment of Desires

If our actions increasingly conform with natural law as a result of establishing Being as the foundation of our thinking process, then the fulfillment of our desires should also be influenced by the degree of Being reflected in our lives. Our desires are rooted in our thoughts. It stands to reason that persons functioning from this field of all possibilities will experience fewer encumbrances to the fulfillment of their desires. And those desires will spontaneously mirror the value of Being and therefore automatically be of optimum value to both the individual and to humanity.

Flashing back to Chapter 3, Deepak Chopra, M.D. reminds us "In the subatomic world, there are no objects. Only oscillating possibilities. And all these possibilities exist simultaneously." This is an intriguing consideration. All possibilities existing at once...a smorgasbord of selections, with the quality of the selections determined by the level of consciousness making the selection.

As reviewed previously, Being or Divinity rests at the foundation of all creation. It gives rise to creation while maintaining its pure, silent, unmanifested nature. Experiencing this state automatically brings success to all fields of activity, including the manifestation of desires.

We are habitually taught that our abilities, intelligence, and energy are the harbingers of success. But in reality, they are of secondary importance to the value of initiating action from the level of Being.

If we have the ability to perform an action so that the surroundings and circumstances support the action's success, then we'll succeed in obtaining maximum results from an action.

I know this above scenario sounds theoretical, but in fact it is the reality I've been experiencing for the past several years. I almost hesitate to write these words out of fear that somehow I'll 'jinx' the process. But it is a very, very real experience. It consistently seems as if the slightest intention materializes, with little or no effort. And it's not limited to hoping that my favorite meal appears on the dinner table this evening. My personal and professional life over the past few years has experienced a cornucopia of accomplishments, large and small, with seemingly only the barest expenditure of intention and energy.

In fact, this is the hallmark of Being reflected in action... action with the least expenditure of energy. Do less, and accomplish more.

This consistent support of nature certainly doesn't mean that I'm immune to adversity or struggle. At any moment, a meteor could come crashing through the living room ceiling where I'm currently writing this text. But I *am* saying that cosmic calamities are muted and every day challenges diminished when Being is consistently cultured within the nervous system.

Chapter 7: Immanence of Consciousness

> "There is no use trying," she said: "one can't believe impossible things."
>
> "I daresay you haven't had much practice," said the Queen. "When I was your age, I always did it for half-an-hour a day. Why, sometimes I've believed as many as six impossible things before breakfast."
>
> Lewis Carroll
> *Alice in Wonderland*

It is impossible to overstate the significance and implications of this concept of spontaneous right action described in Chapter 6. It represents a complete paradigm shift in the way we perceive religion and, more importantly, in the way we attempt to solve problems as individuals and as a society. Countries spend billions of dollars annually, year after wasteful year, in an attempt to ameliorate or solve the myriad of problems plaguing societies since the advent of civilization. All these resources, regardless of their laudable intent, have targeted their focus on the symptomatic nature of the problem rather than its cause; i.e., humans thinking and functioning from a gross level of awareness. A level of consciousness obscured by a nervous system operating at a severely limited capacity.

The discussion of spontaneous right action shows us how individuals can increasingly function from a field of pure Being, reflecting natural law in every thought, word, and action...spontaneously. We saw how the studies on the impact of collective consciousness...the Maharishi Effect...demonstrate how the square root of one percent of a coherently functioning group can generate significant positive changes throughout the community.

The significance of this fact excites me. The idea that spatial barriers can be transcended when cohesive group action reaches a critical level should ignite anyone who participates in prayer circles, healing circles or meditation groups.

I urge you...I *implore* you...to think about the possibilities. The contrast between this approach to problem solving versus the traditional approach is truly staggering. This knowledge has the potential to transform society completely, and this phase transition in awareness can happen almost overnight. I can think of no other event in the history of mankind that could engender such a momentous positive change for every man, woman and child on Earth. And the beauty of the Maharishi Effect is this transformation can occur through the efforts a minuscule number of people creating group coherence. Compare the cost of funding a permanent home for 8,000 people dedicated to this cause (square root of one percent of the world's population) versus the *trillions* of dollars spent annually by world governments for defense alone!

Why are we so blind to this possibility? For the same reason we're inundated with problems...stress in our individual and collective consciousness. It is almost impossible to perceive any other possibilities that lie outside of this suffocatingly small box. It is as if we spend our entire lifetime under overcast skies, not realizing that the Sun exists on the other side of those ominous clouds.

Psychologists refer to this phenomenon as "the slap." When we look at something from only one point of view...from one part of ourselves...we literally cannot see any other. Later, when we realize there was an alternate point of view, when we see what it was that was overlooked, we feel as though an opposite part of us has slapped us.

However, the Sun is destined to shine! And when it does, it will be as if humankind were awakened from a deep slumber. Everyone will take the warm Sun for granted, believing that it was always there. Only history books will remind us about the history of Earth when humans lived under the spell of the illusion of clouds.

This Sun is the Age of Enlightenment prophesized for thousands of years by many cultures. It is now just beginning to dawn and is prophesized to last a thousand years. Can't see the light yet? It is always darkest before the dawn. But the signs of dawning are everywhere if we care to look...listen for the whispers. At the end of Chapter 4, I wrote that this shift "is opening up science to a paradigm that can finally integrate the realm of Spirit with that of the physical. It is spurring new research on the origins of Creation. It seems that events are establishing the foundation of a grand transformation in society."

A new world view is emerging that bridges body and spirit. And the key is the changing nature of consciousness. Modern science, despite its incredible advances in the physical world, has failed to account for the role of consciousness. Consciousness is an anomaly.

Furthermore, the nearly exclusive focus on material acquisition for personal satisfaction and economic growth as the principle measure of collective prosperity has brought about a sense of emptiness for individuals and is rapidly leading to the destruction of the Earth's living systems and, perhaps, to terminal wars of annihilation.

However, the Sun's rays are beginning to reveal that consciousness in the equation is just as fundamental as space, time and matter and, perhaps, more so. The discussions in previous chapters on nonlocal reality, universal mind and the Maharishi Effect provided some insights into the unique role of consciousness.

This new view of consciousness leads us to a fresh understanding and appreciation of spiritual teachings. This understanding transcends the image of God as the Almighty father-figure of classical religion and reveals instead the God of which the mystics have always spoken, the Godhead shining within every one of us as the light of consciousness.

As I said, it is hard to overstate the magnitude of this change. All the pieces for the new worldview are in place. Nothing new needs to be discovered or revealed. All that is required is for us to put the pieces together and explore the new picture of the cosmos that emerges. The darkness we still perceive prior to this dawning begs the need to pursue this awakening with haste.

To those who believe this change is possible, but destined for some civilization far into the future, examine for a moment the principle of phase transitions in nature. Science has long known that only a small percentage, usually less than one percent, of a biological or chemical system needs to display patterns of coherent functioning before triggering a radical shift in the functioning of the entire organism or structure. They call it a phase transition. And often there is a rapid period of entropy displayed by the system just prior to the transition. I believe this is the entropy we are witness to now...the darkness before the dawn. But science also informs us that if sufficient momentum is not present at the point of transition to trigger order throughout the entire system, the entropy will remain until the transition is expedited. For a society, this can represent a very difficult time.

As I'm writing this chapter in February 2003, the United States and its allies are preparing to go to war against Iraq. For months, war drums have been beating. There is a prevailing sense of doubt over the true intentions of this war and an accepted feeling of impotence to do anything to stop it.

Madness appears to be everywhere, at home and internationally. There are dreams of power and annihilation, of revenge and rage. I sense that many are actually intoxicated by this atmosphere. You see the madness in the White House and in the palaces of Iraq's Saddam Hussein.

You see it in the terrorists currently stalking the world. You see it in the scientists who use their talents to manufacture bombs and other weapons of destruction. You see it in the military that will use these weapons and will sacrifice soldiers and civilians to use them. The madness is reflected in the media that has both glorified and disguised the madness, in the filmmakers who have gleefully entertained us with the gore of battle, in everyone who is making a profit from the business of war. The madness is everywhere.

This is the madness of fear and terror and rage, the madness of the closed heart.

However, it is *crucial* for you to realize that this atmosphere only mirrors the collectively closed hearts of *all* of us. One simply cannot exist without the other.

One national organization is encouraging everyone who recognizes the magnitude of this madness to open the closed hearts of our leaders by inundating them with the graphic stories of the war experiences of our fathers and sons. But this well-intentioned endeavor completely ignores the underlying cause of closed hearts and the reality that our collective hearts contribute to the malaise. We look into the mirror to judge our leaders and we see ourselves!

Chapter 5's references to this collective intent bear repeating. I wrote, "We live in a world of collective consent. The conditions of war and suffering on a large-scale mirror the elements that make such conditions possible on a small scale. Sometimes consciously, sometimes not, we consent to expressions of our group-will in ways that we may never suspect. On levels that we may not even be aware of, our thoughts, attitudes and actions toward one another each day contribute to the collective beliefs that 'agree' to the wars and suffering of the world."

"For example," I wrote, "the creation of a wartime mentality of expecting and preparing for conflict in our international world can *happen only if we allow for such conflict in our personal lives.* As we live individual episodes of "defending ourselves" in romance and personal relationships, "outsmarting" others in our schools and "out-strategizing" co-workers and competitors, quantum physics reminds us that these individual expressions of our lives pave the way for similar expressions, amplified by many orders of magnitude, in another time and place. To know peace in our world, we must become peace in our lives."

But how do we open closed hearts? How do we become peace in our lives? The answer is the Maharishi Effect. I refer again to those statistically significant studies demonstrating that groups of people practicing the TM-Sidhi Program have a predictable and measurable effect on the quality of life based on the field effect of the group meditation.

I previously wrote "This is where the application of such studies becomes crucial in global efforts to bring peace to our world. If we view conflict, aggression and war in our outer world as indicators of stress in our collective consciousness, then relieving collective stress should relieve global tensions." Again… the words of Maharishi Mahesh Yogi, founder of Transcendental Meditation ™; "All occurrences of violence, negativity, conflict crisis or problems in any society are just the expression of the growth of stress in collective consciousness. When the level of stress becomes sufficiently great, it bursts out into large-scale violence, war and civil uprising necessitating military action." The beauty of the field effect is that *when stress is relieved within a group the effects are registered beyond the immediate group,* into a larger area.

In addition, if the Maharishi Effect is valid in terms of its collective impact on society, doesn't it make sense that its *primary* impact will occur at the level of *individual* consciousness? In fact, numerous scientific studies and personal experiences indicate this is exactly what occurs.

By effortlessly establishing Being as the foundation of our thoughts...and thoughts always precede action...we perform action based on thoughts expressed at the source of Being. It increasingly ensures the performance of right action in our lives... spontaneously.

As previously stated, I'm obviously a strong proponent of the TM-Sidhi Program. I have over 30 years of experience with the techniques and the tradition. And I'm often asked if TM is only way to enhance collective consciousness? Of course not. The experiences of the mystics alone provide extensive evidence of other doors. (See Chapter 12.) But I not aware of any other modality focused on altering consciousness that exceeds TM's systematic, effortless nature, supported by literally hundreds of physiological, psychological and societal studies verifying its impact. And, for me, one of TM's most salient features is its roots...the ancient Vedas, where the fundamental knowledge was originally cognized directly from the field of Perfect Being by enlightened sages. There is absolutely no doubt in my mind that the TM-Sidhi Program represents the very highest knowledge available to mankind at this time in our history.

The intelligence in the Universe and the *immanence* of consciousness are becoming part of our cosmology. I love this word...immanence. It is such an appropriate and beautiful word. It means 'the presence of God pervading all creation.'

Chapter 8: God the Cosmic Popcorn Popper

> The exclusivism of there being only one way in
> which we can be saved, the idea that there is a
> single religious group that is in sole possession
> of the truth…that is the world as we know it that
> must pass away.
>
> People feel panicky at the thought that we might
> all have something in common, that they are
> giving up some exclusive hold on the truth.
>
> Joseph Campbell

Chapters 5 and 6 establish a significant foundation for
understanding why life is perceived by so many as a constant
struggle. It should be clearer by now that the basis for
suffering is lack of contact with, and the infusion of, Being
into our individual and collective consciousness. The
discussion of the Maharishi Effect and the supporting studies
validating its legitimacy should begin to point us in the
direction of understanding the importance of creating a home
for Being in our lives via the daily practice of
Transcendental Meditation. Only then will the laudable
intentions of all religions begin to bear fruit with a deepening
personal experience of God's true nature…Love.

What is the alternative? What reasoning can you give to
provide a more substantial position for addressing our
individual and societal ills? Does this approach, to
"meditate," sound too Pollyannaish? No more than
believing that the futile attempts made thus far have been
anything but marginally effective. Refer back to Chapter 5
and the impact of group coherence and its statistical
relevance. It's either valid or it isn't. If it is, then it represents
a revolutionary departure from standard approaches to
problem solving that address the problem on the level of the
problem rather than at its root…impaired consciousness.

Water the root of a tree and all components of the tree flourish…we don't just spray water on the leaves and expect results. But we've become so accustomed to accepting these problems as an inevitable part of life. I understand the difficulty in believing that something this simple could have such profound results.

Over the past 3,000 years, more than 8,000 major peace treaties have been signed, with the aim of ending or preventing war. Each of these treaties survived, on average, just nine years.

In 1920, the League of Nations was founded to ensure that World War I would be "the war to end all wars." Less than 20 years later, World War II erupted. In 1945, the United Nations was established, again to end international conflict once and for all. Since 1945, there have been more than 186 wars, resulting in the loss of millions of lives and unspeakable human suffering. International organizations have been powerless to prevent aggression. History repeatedly shows that violence begets violence. Neither weapons, political negotiations, treaties, or agreements have ever succeeded in creating lasting peace…we have 3,000 years of evidence.

As this is written, the Carter Center for Peace Studies in Atlanta is monitoring a total of 112 conflicts throughout the world, many of them based on conflicting ethnic claims. These ethnic divisions are the bitter harvest of the distortions of religious teachings planted long ago. When religious rights are demanded on the basis of literal interpretations of religious tenants instead of as symbols of the heart and spirit, a bitterly divided world arises with the inevitability of great tragedy.

How can we look at this picture of a parochial God and create a bridge to a broader understanding of God and His intentions? How can we begin to feel comfortable with perceiving a God who more realistically reflects the universal attributes all religions traditionally assign to Him?

This can be a long chasm to cross on this bridge, but I think the destination is worth it.

Let's start here.

Science seems to have surpassed religion in delivering awe. How is it that no major religion has looked at the Universe and proclaimed: "This is better than we thought! The Universe is much bigger than our prophets said, grander, more elegant. God must be even greater than we dreamed?" Instead they say, "No, no, no! My God is a little god, and I want him to stay that way." Any religion that stressed the magnificence of the Universe might be able to draw forth reserves of reverence and awe hardly tapped by the conventional faiths. Sooner or later, such a religion will probably emerge.

I often re-read Chapters 1 and 2 just for the fun of it. They describe the size of the Universe and strongly infer that millions, if not billions, of ensouled civilizations inhabit it. To my reckoning, it should be difficult for anyone to read these two chapters and still adhere to the belief that humankind is alone in the Universe.

I particularly appreciate the quote at the beginning of Chapter 2 by Monsignor Balducci, Special Emissary to the Vatican. The Monsignor wrote, "It is illogical and a bit arrogant to believe we are the only beings in God's creation. It is both logical and desirable that "they" exist, since all that God creates gives glory to God the Creator." I especially like his logic that it only makes *sense* that "they" exist. Why wouldn't an all-loving God want to expand His creation "since all that God creates gives glory to God the Creator?"

Father George Coyne, a Jesuit priest and astronomer who heads up the Vatican Observatory, states "In the Augustinian tradition that God is absolute goodness, there is almost a necessity for goodness to reproduce itself, to pour itself out."

But if we're willing to take Monsignor Balducci's and Father Coyne's leap of faith that it only makes sense that "they" exist, it also requires another significant leap...one can't exist without the other. Accepting the reality of other civilizations as part of God's love and creation forces us to accept the larger reality that God plays an active role in *their* lives, too. And this loving role probably includes periodic incarnations of other Sons of God to assist in *their* evolution, closely mirroring Jesus' role on Earth. It would only make sense, wouldn't it?

For the sake of illustrating this point, imagine for a moment that humankind is the *only* ensouled civilization in the Milky Way Galaxy, despite Carl Sagan's estimate that up to one million civilizations may exist in our Galaxy alone. Let's also assume for a moment that Jesus of Nazareth has been the *only* incarnation of the Father-God on Earth.

Chapter 1, *The Great Designer*, discusses the reality of the existence of perhaps 120 billion *other* galaxies. Therefore, let's apply here the same formula discussed above...each of these galaxies contains only one ensouled civilization saved by only one Savior. I don't think these minimum assumptions require a serious stretch of anyone's imagination.

So, for the sake of this exercise, we have now accepted the size of the Universe, the number of its galaxies, and the contention that each of these galaxies has only one ensouled civilization. We are also now inclined to accept the possibility that an all-loving God would probably want to extend to them the same degree of love and concern extended to us on Earth by providing them with an incarnation of Himself.

If you can accept these possibilities up to this point, are you not compelled to accept the existence of literally *billions* of Saviors? One Savior per galaxy! If so, what does that say about our possessive attitude concerning what constitutes religious truth? Are there 120 billion different religions practiced in the Universe? Did God make different rules for different planets or galaxies? Or did perhaps the God that governs all of us create a universal natural law for the entire Universe?

If so, does this natural law emanate from a field of Being that lies at the foundation of *all* existence in the Universe? And does the nonlocal reality of this field unite us all in a common heritage? And wouldn't it make sense that this heritage would be the formless Supreme Being of absolute, eternal nature, the Divinity that rests silently at the core of Being, of all Creation? And wouldn't such an all-loving Supreme Being acknowledge the need for *all* civilizations to have Him periodically incarnate in a personal form, with a specific nature, exhibiting the many attributes we usually associate with the Son of God?

And wouldn't these attributes include the worship of Sons of God in a manner reflecting the time and culture in which He manifested? And wouldn't these Sons of God have made sure that Their original disciples received and disseminated Their teachings in a form that taught the existence of Their universal nature and a means to assimilate it at the level of Being?

I sincerely believe that the answer to the last seven questions is an unequivocal *yes*!

Eventually, all of us will grow out of our state of confusion and accept the reality of a Universe filled with life. And sentient beings throughout the Universe will recognize our common destiny and our Divine heritage. When this happens, we will not be at the end of our evolutionary journey. All the evidence suggests that we will then only *begin* to recognize the meaning of infinity and, thus, of the truly long-term consequences to our Father's gift of life to us.

And the evolutionary process may never end. And why should it? Why would God want to stop the expansion of His own existence? Doesn't it make sense to say that He will want to grow in loving variety throughout all eternity? I see nothing to indicate that God is planning on eventually closing shop.

And our discussion thus far has been limited to God's presence in *this* Universe. As glimpsed in Chapter 1, there are credible scientific theories that support the notion that our incomprehensible Universe may be one of *many* such Universes. And why not? It is easy for me to fathom that a God who is the expression of unbounded, unconditional Love would want to spread that Love around. And as discussed in Chapter 3, some scientists believe that our Universe was created in an infinitesimal fraction of a second from a single kernel of virtual matter. Therefore, I can perceive a God who is a virtual cosmic popcorn popper, popping out multiple Universes maybe for the shear fun of creating!

I sometimes fantasize about the expanded levels of consciousness that must be prevalent on many of these galactic planets that are perhaps thousands of years ahead of our civilization, and thus have had the time to evolve to higher states of awareness. How enlivening it must be to live in an atmosphere where war and inhumanity to others has been relegated to history. We take for granted that our 21st century civilization rests at the vanguard of civilized and enlightened behavior, conveniently overlooking the slaughter of 100 million of our earthly siblings over the past 100 years.

If God's creation of billions of ensouled civilizations on billions of planets gives glory to God the Creator, it's fun to conceive of the billions and trillions of examples that must abound of the creativity exhibited by His created souls. Think metaphorically of the billions of Sistine Chapels, the billions of Beethoven Fifth Symphonies and the billions of children growing up knowing no distinction between their poetic dream world and everyday reality.

Section II:
The Journey Continues

Chapter 9: Bottled God

> I have come to the conclusion that whether or not a person is a religious believer does not matter much. Far more important is that they be a good human being.
>
> Dalai Lama
> *Ethics for the New Millennium*

Mankind's attempts through the ages to define God are a fascinating study. From the earliest civilizations to the present, God has attracted a myriad of attributes, each reflecting the cultural conventions of the time.

When we look back at so-called "primitive" civilizations, we often assume a superior attitude when we compare their "pagan" Gods to our more comfortable and modern definitions. But are our religious customs really that much different from our "pagan" ancestors?

God, as the Creator of this unbounded Universe, has often been captured, bottled and corked by much of mankind as a child fills a bottle from the ocean and proudly proclaims its contents *as* the ocean. This reality has been a consistent source of personal frustration, a perpetual test of my ability to separate judgment from observation.

In fact, this chapter was originally the *first* chapter written for this book. And this chapter's title, Bottled God, was the book's *initial* title. This frustration increasingly urged me to begin writing about our need to more clearly understand what God is...and isn't. As an avid student of the mystical school, I found solace in St. John of the Cross's concern that some people, retarded in their spiritual life, "still think of God as little children and speak of God as little children, and feel and experience God as little children." In other words, he wanted people to get rid of children's ideas of God and to grow up!

As Christian mystic Bernadette Roberts writes, "If we have any concepts of what God is, certainly it should be changing and expanding as we ourselves grow and change. This is the very nature of our life's movement: to expand, to open up and blossom."

I realize that encouraging people to go beyond their parochial ideas of God was a tall order. But I found it difficult to fathom that most people feel that they are in a "special" spiritual group or religion, one that God smiles upon exclusively. My beliefs expressed earlier in this book concerning our boundless Universe, teeming with countless galaxies inhabited by innumerable civilizations, only added fuel to this dilemma.

As previously described herein, the Creator has created an almost un-definable, magnificent Universe where boundaries are unknown to man. A Universe so boundless, teeming with countless galaxies containing billions of star systems, which in turn claim heritage to trillions of planets.

Mankind is a part of this magnificent creation. We are Sparks emanating from the Divine Flame, Who created light from darkness, matter from Absolute Being.

The power of such a Creator is unfathomable. A Creator of tremendous contrasts. Creating the unfathomable, while simultaneously infusing Creation with an unfathomable degree of Love for His Creation. Love, the energy that excited the darkness into Light. Love, the cosmic breath of Absolute Being, the prana permeating beingness to create the Universe and its countless manifestations of the Creator.

There have been many theories trying to explain why God fashioned Creation. Most theorists have the intelligence to realize that their theories are only that. Who could possibly be so conceited as to believe he understands the mind of God? Even my exhortation that God's "Love for His

Creation" powers the Universe is only a feeble attempt to make the unknowable, knowable. And it is truly impossible to convey in words the true meaning of 'Love' as it applies to God's Love. It transcends description or definition.

But, there does seem to be an almost universal belief that Creation is not the result of some complicated intention or even a cumbersome process. Einstein wrote, "God does not play dice with the universe." As expressed several chapters ago, it is easy to fathom that a God who is the expression of unbounded, unconditional Love would want to spread that Love around. Maybe for the sheer fun of creating! And the latest theories of quantum physics strongly favor a process of creation that involved, and continues to involve, a beautiful symmetry and simplicity...infinitesimally small vibrating strings excited by an unmanifest consciousness.

Man is a product of God's Love. Can we ever begin to understand the depth and breadth of this Love? Prior chapters attempted to equate an increased experience of Love with the ability to transcend habitually to the field of Absolute Being and to assimilate Being into our awareness. But despite our attempts to understand, despite our limited understanding of the limitless...we are still so quick to confine the Creator and His Love to Bottled God.

Don't most of us purchase Bottled God? Don't we proclaim to understand the totality of God, and then promptly fill our religious bottle from the Creator's ocean and then self-righteously proclaim that our Bottled God represents God's true nature? And, don't we deny ourselves or anyone else to remove the cork of our Bottled God, lest we lose Him or expose Him to contamination from someone else's brand of Bottled God? There is no sequestering of spirit any more than there would be a sequestering of family love. Love is universal, and it is part of all humanity.

And haven't established religions done a superlative job teaching us that to question the word of God is to invite His wrath? This is a sad commentary on most religions.

Promulgating the belief that we are separate from God and only through His Divine Grace can we ever hope to reunite with Him and, in the meantime, live in fear of God's tribulation if we question this tenant of separation. This message of fear is one of the most debilitating and tragic legacies of religions, abandoning millions to the shadows of the illusion that we are unworthy of God's unconditional love. This is an oxymoron if I ever heard one…unworthy of unconditional love. And history cries out with the accounts of millions of deaths discharged in God's name.

I certainly understand that we're dealing with historical value systems and cultural differences on this planet, where literally billions of humans put together spiritual information and placed it into systems that work for them. I'm not immune to this influence. I also think that each system that has high integrity and searches for the "God within" is greatly honored. It's a grand search.

But in this searching process, and within the scope of history, humans have bottled God. It is understandable how this happened. However, in the bottling process, a belief has developed that states "God smiles on us and us *only*."

Most of us were taught that we were created in the image and likeness of God. Therefore, if I am worthy of my parent's love with whom I share an intimate emotional and genetic relationship, am I not even more worthy of the Love of my heavenly Father whose Divinity I share?

I think that knowing God is perhaps the greatest personal challenge anyone will face in life. And the greatest obstacle to relishing this challenge is the feeling of unworthiness. That is why most people choose to know theories about God instead of knowing their loving Father directly. It is unfortunate that many theological agendas enforce the idea of unworthiness. Thus, people are trapped. God is a power and love greater than words, greater than anything that could ever be put into words. Yet, what Father would not welcome the presence of His own child?

How incredibly vain we can be! How incredibly insulting we can be to the Creator! (Although I assume it is impossible to insult, offend or hurt God in any manner.) How incredibly *fearful* we are! Fearing the retribution of our Bottled God if we should dare to attempt to perceive Him in any way other than what is represented in our bottle. A bottle typically filled for us by our parents and our religious institutions, our culture.

As we've already learned, astronomers and other scientists are threatening the comfort level of our Bottled God. They tell us that mankind cannot possibly be the sole heir to the Creator's manifestations. That it is almost statistically impossible to conceive a Universe that does not contain literally millions of other intelligent civilizations.

So, we are not alone. But how could we have ever been so naïve to believe otherwise? How could we, on the one hand, proclaim to understand elements of the totality of the Creator, and, on the other hand, limit the expression of His Love to the creation of humankind alone? Doesn't a true definition of Love literally *beg* to reflect itself into as much of Creation as possible, as Monsignor Balducci suggests? If God were synonymous with Love, wouldn't He want to infuse His Love into as many manifestations of His Creation as possible? Indeed, if God were Love, would not every element of His Creation be a spark of His Divine Love? How could it be anything else?

If we accept this premise, then why are we so quick to make the un-definable, definable? Why are we so absolute in our belief that *our* definition of the aspirations of the Creator is the correct definition?

There is a woman who gives birth to twins. One is a boy, the other is a girl. Which one do you think will be her favorite, and which one is she going to cast off? Of course, the answer is neither. They are loved equally, beyond measure. They are her family. And thus it is so with God. All humanity is God's family, loved equally and universally and unconditionally. If

God is our Father, then why would He throw away most of His children and smile only on a few?

But why, then, do we cling so tenaciously to our brand of Bottled God? The answer stems from the reality that each brand has truly felt the Love of Spirit added to their bottle, giving rise to a validation that God has smiled on them specifically. And they're right. God *has* loved and blessed them.

But if they would only sample the other brands, they would discover the same uniqueness. They would find the same integrity and love. God's Love is universal because we are all a part of God's family. Special smiles experienced by one brand do not devalue the others.

Please understand that I'm trying hard not to judge. These are my observations and a plea to listen to the whispers and understand a higher reality. God's Love of His family is absolute. We are loved without measure. That is the relationship of integrity between humanity and God. And this should be the goal of the relationship between humans…between Bottle and Bottle. This integrity of spiritual relationships *has* to change in order for humanity to move into the long-prophesized age of peace.

There are a lot of brands of Bottled God. There are 5,000 to 6,000 sects of Christianity alone. Some brands are similar, other distinctly different, depending primarily on our culture. And, it's important to recognize that Bottled God serves a beneficial role. These benefits are familiar to all of us.

However, can a single, omnipotent Creator honestly be represented by all brands of Bottled God? How can one brand, with an ingredient that claims that their God loves you unconditionally, sentence you to eternal damnation if you violate one of His more serious tenants? How can another brand claim that their God will reward them with the riches of heaven if they serve Him on Earth by massacring other humans in His name? Does this sound like God to you? We created different bottles of spiritual isolation to protect our culture. But this protection has very little to do with God and a great deal to do with humans. It's time we use our integrity discernment.

But wait. Haven't we stated that we are probably not alone in the cosmos? How will the contents of our Bottled God impact other ensouled civilizations? Is it conceivable that the Creator has also manifested to them? Are their brands of BG similar to ours? Different? How different?

It is highly probable that the Creator's emanations of Love throughout the Universe have been packaged by other civilizations as well. Packaging serves a purpose. It can nourish us. It can provide a sense of purpose when we feel purposeless. It can serve as a loving hand to support and guide us on our journey to discover the uniqueness of our individuality and the contribution of this individuality to the collective upliftment of others.

However, it is conceivable that other civilizations have managed to transcend the limitations of BG. To return to the unbounded Ocean of Love. Does this possibility register an ever-so-faint whisper deep within your awareness? In an unguarded moment, can't you feel a stirring within that beckons you to a deeper experience of the Creator's Love? I sometimes listen to this whisper, refusing to recognize any shadows of fear that may be lurking nearby to remind me of the dire consequences of allowing myself to feel this wondrous feeling...to listen to my soul's deepest and most profound music.

Dare to allow yourself to breathe more of the Creator's gift of Love. Breathe It in through your heart, not your head. Allow yourself to loosen the cork of your religious allegiance for just a brief moment...allow just a little portion of your Bottle to seep back into the Ocean...actually imagine it flowing...to become *refreshed* in the bliss of God's limitless Love. It's okay to refill your Bottle again, but you may now notice that your Bottle is a little larger. It holds more. Its ingredients are richer, more fulfilling. There is less fear associated with the idea of venturing beyond the rim of your Bottle again.

And when you hear that inner whisper again, when fear is asleep, tiptoe to the Ocean again for refreshment. The Ocean is limitless. You never have to be afraid of losing the Love you have…there is always more. Wouldn't perfect Love endow perfect trust?

Respect those who have assisted you in filling your vessel, even if they insist on keeping the cork tight. "It is a lifelong process to become patient and make peace with the notion that every person is just where he or she needs to be," writes Deepak Chopra. Just remember the truth that whispers to all of us, if we will only listen. This truth declares that God and fear are completely and universally incompatible, on Earth and throughout the Universe.

Fear is anathema to God, to Love. Experience Love *separate* from fear and experience more and more of God's true essence. Fear is a shadow…it doesn't exist in the Light…it *can't* exist in the Light. Any action taken with fear as a companion is doomed to cover God with clouds of ignorance.

The process of moving through the shift…coming out from under the illusion of fear and facing the Light of transformation…the connection we have, the genetic connection with our family…sometimes we look at ourselves as a solitary being struggling forward in carrying our personal crosses.

But there is only one cross…loss of the knowledge that we are one with God. There is only one consciousness, God's consciousness, and we see ourselves through the color of whatever veil we've created by the ego identifying with our illusions. We often feel the strong need to bring others along…to "save" others…often feeling this has to be accomplished by direct contact.

Quantum physics teaches us that past and future are illusions. There is only the now. The challenge is to go beyond the intellectual acceptance of this reality and cross the bridge to experiencing the now and using that experience as a springboard to the next moment, to the next and the next, without interruption.

It has never been about what's coming in the future…it's about what's right now.

What keeps us from experiencing the now in its fullness? How can we enter the flow experientially? How can we bypass our impatience? What is the one, single most uplifting message I can provide to you to help illuminate this desire to experience more fully the now? It is this. *Ultimately, God can only be contacted and experienced in His fullness through transcendence…otherwise it's mood-making.* And there's "a whole lotta mood-makin' goin on!" Merely thinking about God won't do.

Paramahansa Yogananda, in *Man's Eternal Quest*, writes eloquently on this value of transcendence. "But greater than activity, devotion, or reason, is meditation. To meditate truly is to focus solely on Spirit. This is esoteric mediation. It is the highest form of activity that man can perform, and it is the most balanced way to find God. If you work all the time you may become mechanical and lose Him in preoccupation with your duties; and if you seek Him only through discriminate thought you may lose Him in the labyrinths of endless reasoning; and if you cultivate only devotion for God, your development may become merely emotional. But meditation combines and balances all these approaches."

The unknown 14th century mystic who authored *The Cloud of Unknowing* offers another perspective of meditation. "It is, of course, a great paradox that we should help people precisely by forgetting them (referring to the transcending process where all thought is by-passed). Therefore, firmly reject all clear ideas however pious or delightful. For I tell you this; one loving blind desire for God alone is…more helpful to your friends, both living and dead, than anything else you could do."

Because of its abstract nature, the study of this transcendent field, Being, has been shrouded in mysticism. Consequently, for countless generations, the ordinary man has been deprived of the great advantages of experiencing Being, our birthright. *But now anyone can begin to experience the bottomless well of God's Love via the simple yet profound practice of Transcendental Meditation.*

But isn't TM a religion?

Transcendental Meditation came from a tradition that is the oldest spiritual tradition in existence. It predates Christianity by several thousand years. To equate TM with any religion would be a mistake. Meditation is the means for gaining spiritual enlightenment because it systematically destroys everything within us that stands between us and God. *It is the state of spiritual enlightenment that is the inspiration and the foundation upon which the various religions were established.* Please read this paragraph again. I think it is essential that you understand it.

The original teachings of enlightened masters and avatars (or incarnations of God), though they may be different, *do not contradict each other.* They are all valid and they are all true, at least they were when they were originally taught. Unfortunately, teachings are given by enlightened teachers to unenlightened students who promptly begin to twist the teachings into self-serving viewpoints that ultimately lead to the belief that they've cornered the market on truth.

Meditation is a spiritual technique, not a religion. What do you think will happen when a Christian, a Buddhist, a Hindu, or a Jew reach enlightenment? What will be the differences in their religious beliefs? *The answer is none.* All of the beliefs that were mistaken, or only partially true, will have been replaced with direct knowledge.

There is a woman who gives birth to twins. One is a boy, the other is a girl. They are both loved beyond measure. They are a piece of the whole of the Father...Sparks from the Divine Flame. There are no favorites, and the family does not smile on one and not another. For all are equal in God's eyes.

Chapter 10: To Hell With It

> I cannot imagine a God who rewards and
> punishes the objects of his creation, a God whose
> purposes are modeled after our own...a God, in
> short, who is but a reflection of human frailty.
>
> Albert Einstein

> What do you have to fear? Nothing. Whom do
> you have to fear? No one. Why? Because
> whoever has joined forces with God obtains
> three great privileges: omnipotence without
> power, intoxication without wine, and life
> without death.
>
> St. Francis of Assisi

I don't think anything has captured the imagination of
humanity more completely than the idea of hell. *The* place to
which God condemns those who have not obeyed His law.

It was the first brick that came loose for me as a young
Catholic. I just couldn't reconcile Church teachings of an all-
loving, compassionate and forgiving God on one hand with a
vengeful God on the other. Remember the statement in the
Introduction about contemplating eternity? Trying to
imagine existence as never ending can give you a real case of
the 'willies.' Now add an eternal *hell* to the equation...it
soon became impossible to reconcile, despite my intimate
bond to the Church. Okay, sin deserves punishment, I
reasoned. As ye sow, so shall you reap. But what sin or sins
could anyone commit that would warrant an *eternity* of
unimaginable torment?

But the histories of most religions speak of hell. Frightening,
gruesome paintings of this horrific place appear in frescoes
on the ceilings and walls of churches all over the world. And

equally upsetting images of hell adorn the pages of catechisms and Sunday-school booklets given to little children…the better to scare them with!

At a Papal audience held by Pope John Paul II at the Vatican in July 1999, he stated that "improper use of biblical pictures must not create psychosis or anxiety." The biblical descriptions of hell are symbolic and metaphorical. He said that the "inextinguishable fire" and "the burning oven" the Bible speaks of "indicate the complete frustration and vacuity of a life without God." Hell is a state of separation from God, he explained, a state caused not by a punishing God, but rather *self-induced.* It is not God's function to administer retribution or to punish anyone, and the Pope made that clear in his audience.

We on Earth have a strange preoccupation with evil. Not the everyday evil we see around us in our lives, but an evil we *can't* see…a supernatural force that is so easy to blame when we don't want to face our own failings on Earth. Some people actually believe in an all-encompassing force of evil that is so powerful it rivals the power of God.

Most of us have been taught that if we're not good, or if we don't practice the 'right' religion, God will send our sorry butt straight to hell, without much thought or consideration. Or, at a minimum, we'll experience the fire of Purgatory until we've suffered enough to sufficiently atone for the minor sins we've committed before God will welcome us into Heaven. (I can still recall my fourth grade nun's admonition to use every line on our writing tablet or face the fire of Purgatory for the wasted paper!) The threat of damnation is propagated by ill-informed…though probably well-meaning…people who want to believe that if someone wrongs us, hurts us or does despicable things on Earth, then off to a fiery punishment they'll go, sent by a vengeful, righteous God.

It may be a soothing thought; that those who made us suffer will suffer themselves, but we have forgotten that there is a force more powerful than our own, with a much better command over right and wrong and a decidedly better perspective than we can ever have on Earth. These same people, who rant and rave that the punishment for wrongs on Earth should be swift and mighty, have forgotten perhaps the most fundamental belief they hold...justice is the domain of God. I am baffled when I hear people say that God knows us, loves us and understands our struggles, yet in the same breath say that God will turn around and punish us if the relationship gets a little bumpy.

But doesn't the Bible warn us of the dangers of eternal damnation?

Yes. In fact, some fundamentalist sects are quick to remind us of St. John's admonition in 3:3 to be "born again" or risk being denied entrance into the Kingdom, which leaves us with only one alternative location.

I'm not a Biblical scholar. But the New Testament authors didn't compose their gospels until well after Christ's death. Therefore, we have to question whether their memory was capable of capturing the literal words of Christ. And we need to be concerned with the cultural milieu and idiosyncrasies of the language of that era and society. And the gospels were originally conveyed orally. Then they were recorded in Aramaic, subsequently translated into Hebrew by others, then into Greek, Latin and 14th century English and, eventually, into modern English and a multitude of other world languages. Linguists write of the many challenges associated with translating languages while trying to maintain the integrity of meaning, syntax and an abundance of other linguistic variables. (Additional insights into the loss of knowledge created by the gathering of biblical books are presented in the next chapter.)

Is there a role for Divine inspiration to overcome these obstacles? Perhaps. But does it smoothly transcend through the many translations and their associated nuances to give us a fully accurate rendition of Christ's original messages? Probably not.

Even assuming that Divine inspiration is present, the inspired passages are seldom clear enough to create a consensus on their meaning, even for those who subscribe to the literal interpretation school of thought. Take for example the passage we just used; "Except a man be born again, he cannot see the Kingdom of God." Literalists interpret 'born again' as accepting Jesus Christ as Lord and Savior, the Kingdom of Heaven as a real place and Hell as the destination for those who abdicate the directive. Non-literalists have a range of interpretations for born again, with "the Kingdom of Heaven is within you" as its location and Hell as the alternative as simply a ludicrous contention.

In John 14:6, Christ states "I am the way, the truth, and the life: no man cometh unto the Father, but by me." Jesus meant, never that he was the sole Son of God, but that no man can attain the unqualified Absolute, the transcendent Father *beyond* creation, until he has first manifested the 'Son' or activating Christ Consciousness *within* creation. Jesus, who had achieved entire oneness with that Christ Consciousness, identified himself with it inasmuch as his own ego had long since been dissolved.

A form of spiritual cowardice leads many worldly people to believe comfortably that only one man was the Son of God. "Christ was uniquely created," they reason, "so how can I, a mere mortal, emulate Him?" But all men have been divinely created, and must someday obey Christ's command" Be ye therefore perfect, even as your Father which is in heaven is perfect." (Matthew 5:48)

In I Corinthians 15:31, St. Paul writes, "I die daily." Since he didn't *literally* die daily, what are we to assume about his dictum? If his daily death is just a metaphor, then he must have been born again *every* day, which may also be a metaphor. I personally subscribe to the contention that St. Paul's daily spiritual exercises included a means to transcend physical and mental activity, bringing the body's metabolic rate to a virtual standstill, thus feeling as if he died. This is a very similar phenomena described by mystics of all traditions as well as by long-term practitioners of meditation.

Now, back to hell.

I remember my father, a deeply devout Roman Catholic, discussing the idea of hell with me as a teenager. Despite his strict allegiance to Church doctrine, I think the permanence and agony of hell caused him some bewilderment. He said that as a parent, it was inconceivable that he could punish one of his children for committing a major infraction by holding their hand in an open flame for even a few seconds. He also said that we are taught that God loves His children even more than their Earthly parents. So the idea that God could inflict such a punishment was difficult for him to comprehend.

In later years, one evening about a year before his death at age 88, my father and I had what was perhaps the most intimate conversation we ever shared. Again, it was over Catholic doctrine; more specifically his great concern over my lack of allegiance *to* it. He once told my brother that the saddest day of his life would be the day one of his children "fell away" from the Church. (I am one of nine.) With this concern in mind, I asked him if he believed that God would condemn my soul to hell if I died in an automobile accident on the way home that evening. He quickly answered "no," which certainly put my mind to rest; what a momentous albatross it would be for a parent to carry such a burden. But many do.

Two of my most cherished gifts in this life were my presence at the death of both of my parents; my mother in 1998 and dad in 2001. This is not a macabre statement, as anyone who has had the experience can testify. 'Spiritual' does not even begin to describe the moment.

With dad, I had spent the night in his hospital room, sleeping on a day bed. He had experienced a stroke five days before. As morning approached, I heard his snoring become fainter and fainter. Knowing his departure was close, I sat on his bed, cradling his head in my lap, gently stroking his forehead, whispering to him that it was okay to go. And he went. In hindsight, I felt that it was providence that I was the child present at his death. It gave me a profoundly deep connection with him…it seemed to vanish any prior consternation between us over my taking a different spiritual path in life. I'll cherish the moment forever.

The Bible speaks of sowing what we reap. True. But I would go so far as to state that God has *never* punished a soul…ever! God, who knows us at the very core of our being, understands the errors we create, the evil we do and the failures that move us off the path in life. However, despite how far we cast ourselves away from our purpose on Earth, God will never abandon us. God doesn't force us to own up to our failings…*we* will do it in the hereafter because of the irresistible peace and love that abounds there, and *all* souls want to be loved.

While knowing that there is no punishment in the next life sounds very good for those who have done terrible things on Earth, it's important to understand that no one escapes having to reconcile the sins we commit on Earth. When we have wasted our opportunities to grow spiritually or, worse, spent our time here making others suffer, we will enter the hereafter to understand firsthand how our actions hurt others, and how damaging these actions were to our spiritual growth.

Thus, we won't experience the full spiritual benefit of the beauty of God until we know we have earned it. *Nothing* is unforgivable, and no matter how bad the deed, the slow process of undoing the damage and moving closer to God is available to all souls who truly want it. I'm sorry if this explanation is disappointing to some, but I think it's an important part of our spiritual education. I know we want compensation from those who have wronged society and us, but we need to keep to our own purpose and trust God.

Unfortunately, many people will always believe in hell, and in a God who would send them there, as long as they believe that God is like man...ruthless, self-serving, unforgiving, and vengeful.

Neale Donald Walsch, author of *Conversations with God*, a book purporting to record his direct conversations with God, quotes God as saying; "evil is that which you *call* evil. Yet even that I love, for it is only when you know what you call evil can you know good, and only when you know what you call the work of the devil can you know and do the work of God. I do not love hot more than cold. It is all relative. It is all a part of what is. I do not love "good" more than I love "bad." Hitler went to Heaven. When you understand this, you will understand God."

Whew!

Mankind has a rich tradition of expressing God's willingness to forgive us for our transgressions. We have experienced this as an aspect of Divine Love...moving us closer and closer to the truth of both Love and Divinity itself.

One of the most famous stories of forgiveness that has moved us closer to the truth of God's love and Divinity is the account of Jesus forgiving the man on the cross beside Him, revealing the eternal truth that *no one is condemned who seeks God*. This means that no one is ever condemned, because everyone ultimately seeks God, whether they call it that or not.

Hell is the experience of the separation from God. Yet anyone who doesn't want to experience eternal separation doesn't have to. The great desire for reunion with God produces it.

Now listen closely...the next statement may loosen several bricks. Forgiveness is *never* necessary. It isn't necessary since no true offense can even be committed against Divinity itself, since Divinity itself is All That Is. Who would forgive whom? And for what? Does the hand forgive the toe for stubbing itself?

Each person, being a product of Divine Mind, is held in that Mind as a perfect idea. Not one of us has to conceive himself. We have been perfectly conceived and are always held in the perfect Mind of God as perfect beings. By having this realization brought to our consciousness via transcending, we can contact the Divine Mind and so re-conceive what God has already conceived for us. This may be what Jesus meant by being "born again." It is the great gift the silence of the transcendence has to offer us. For by contacting the God-Mind, we can think with God-Mind and know ourselves as we are in reality rather than as we have thought ourselves to be.

When our society understands this, we will never again condemn another or ourselves. We will never again embrace a vengeful, angry, damning God who would condemn us to everlasting torture. In that moment, we will relinquish forever our idea of a condemning God, for we'll know that unconditional love could never condemn. Then we'll condemn no one and nothing, either, according to God's directive: Judge not, and neither condemn.

Chapter 11: Here We Go Again

Him that overcometh will I make a pillar in
the temple of my God, and he shall go out
no more.

John, Revelations 3:12

I myself was never not, nor thou, nor all the
princes of the earth; nor shall we ever
hereafter cease to be.

Lord Krishna
Bhagavad-Gita

Most versions of today's Christian religions base their core beliefs on the New Testament; the Holy Bible.

However, few people understand how the Bible came into being. It isn't actually a book at all, but a series of manuscripts, ranging from Genesis to Revelation.

But where did these manuscripts come from? The evolution of Christian thought as expressed through the various manuscripts is a fascinating one. But we'll only touch lightly on it here. There were many early Church historians, or fathers of the Church as they're often called, who wrote accounts and implications of historical events during the time of Christ. But these accounts were loosely organized.

By the early fourth century A.D., it became obvious to many Church fathers that in order to establish a solid and credible foundation for the growth of the Church, a basic frame of reference had to be developed for Christ's teachings. Church fathers clearly perceived the need to gather the various writings from the hinterland and decide what writings represented the basic foundation of Church doctrine.

Consequently, Roman emperor Constantine formed a council of historians and scholars in 325 AD that later became known as the Council of Nicea. Over a period of years, the Council reviewed hundreds of documents and texts, eventually recommending that at least 25 documents be modified or removed from the collection of texts. The Council found many of the works to be redundant. Other manuscripts were so abstract and, in some cases, so mystical that they were believed to be beyond any practical value. (For an engaging insight into these mystical texts, read Gregg Braden's *The Isaiah Effect*.) Additionally, another 20 supporting documents were removed, held in reserve for privileged researchers and select scholars. The remaining texts were condensed, rearranged and edited to give them greater meaning and to make them more accessible to the common reader. Constantine himself edited many of the texts. The result was essentially today's New Testament.

The task was completed in 553 A.D. at the Second Synod Council of Constantinople. And the consequences of removing, or in some cases, altering these manuscripts that detail the Christian heritage remain with us today.

A prime example of one consequence is the principle of reincarnation.

Prior to the Council of Nicea, assorted Church historians accepted and preached a belief in the continual evolution of the soul through many lifetimes as the soul progressed towards perfection or enlightenment.

St. Gregory of Nyssa, 257-332 A.D., wrote "It is absolutely necessary that the soul should be healed and purified, and if it does not take place during its life on earth, it must be accomplished in future lives."

Origen, A.D. 185-254 A.D., whom St. Gregory of Nyssa called "the prince of Christian learning in the third century," and whom St. Jerome later called "the greatest teacher of the Church after the apostles," wrote in Contra Celsum...

Is it not more in conformity with reason that every soul for certain mysterious reasons is introduced into a body, and introduced according to its deserts and former actions?

Is it not rational that souls should be introduced into bodies, in accordance with their merits and previous deeds, and that those who have used their bodies in doing the utmost possible good should have a right to bodies endowed with qualities superior to the bodies of others?

The soul, which is immaterial and invisible in its nature, exists in no material place, without having a body suited to the nature of that place; accordingly, it at one time puts off one body, which was necessary before, but which is no longer adequate in its changed state, and it exchanges it for a second.

In De Principiis, Origen writes "Every soul...comes into this world strengthened by the victories or weakened by the defeats of its previous life."

The belief in reincarnation was outlawed at the Second Synod Council of Constantinople. The council decided that: "If anyone asserts the fabulous pre-existence of souls and shall submit to the monstrous doctrine that follows from it, let him be...excommunicated."

So, what drove Christianity from an era when respected Church fathers embraced the rationality of reincarnation to today's Church where reincarnation is relegated to the domain of snake charmers from the Indian subcontinent? The answer can be reduced to a single word...*control*.

Christianity, as do most religions, contains a strong element of control. Control governed by *fear*. It teaches a doctrine of a God who is to be worshipped *and* feared. It was through fear that the early priests got people to "mend their wicked ways" and "heed the word of the Lord." It was through fear that churches gained, and controlled, their membership. And this dubious legacy continues today.

Let me stop here and state unequivocally that I'm not intentionally "bashing" any religious belief. As I stated in the Introduction, I understand that "your beliefs are very precious to you." The Catholic Church has certainly played a pivotal and cherished role in my own personal spiritual development.

However, I do not subscribe to a doctrine of blind faith. Despite my attraction to the concept of Divine Inspiration as a guiding light in the evolution of both Church doctrine and individual illumination, I'm equally aware that the Church hierarchy through the ages has employed the same less-than-admirable trait often practiced by all of us to impose our will…*control* through *fear*.

I want to distinguish between control for control's sake to preserve the vestiges of power, versus the need to teach the legitimate concept of sowing what we reap. The later is essentially steeped in the importance of treating others as we wish to be treated.

But the former…issuing religious edicts as a tactic to preserve the seat of power…has clearly overshadowed the governance of the Church from its earliest days to the present. And most of these self-serving edicts, such as the removal of the reincarnation of the soul as a central teaching, have little resemblance to the purity of Christ's original teachings.

Many of the infractions generated by the conscious exercise of control are well known. Let's see how they relate to the demise of the role of reincarnation. It's truly a fascinating examination.

From the early Church until today, dogma insisted that God would punish you if you didn't attend church on the Lord's Day. Not going to church was declared a sin. And not just any church. You had to attend one particular church. If you went to a church of a different denomination, even though you were giving praise to God, that was a sin, too. I remember an elementary school nun cautioning the class that it was a sin to sing the Christmas hymn "Away in the Manger" because a "fallen-away" Catholic composed it!

In ages past, people could not imagine a God who might rise above all of this control and fear. So they accepted the teaching to "fear the terrible vengeance of the Lord." It was as if people could not trust themselves to be good, to act appropriately. So they had to create a religion that taught the doctrine of an angry, retributive God in order to keep them in line.

But the idea of reincarnation threw a monkey wrench into that reasoning.

The Church was teaching that you'd better be good or *else*. Then along came the reincarnationists, saying: "You'll have another chance after this life, and another chance after that. And still more chances. So don't worry. Do the best you can, and get on with it."

Naturally, the early Church couldn't hear of such a thing. So it did two things. First, it denounced the doctrine of reincarnation as heretical. Then it created the sacrament of confession. Confession could do for the churchgoer what reincarnation promised. That is, *to give him another chance.*

But there was a clever catch...the absolution of confession couldn't come through directly from God...it had to flow through the priest who gave you "penances" to perform. So now there were two reasons to keep up your Church membership. It worked so well that the Church soon made it a sin *not* to go to confession at least once a year. More rules, with each rule having the power of God's wrath behind it, unless, of course, the sin was confessed. Then the sinner was forgiven by God.

But another problem arose. Sinners figured out that they could do anything wrong as long as they confessed it. Their fear was gone. They confessed their sins once a year, did their penances, were absolved of their sins and went on with their lives. Priests were again losing control over the people. Solution? Recreate fear by inventing Purgatory.

Purgatory was a place similar to hell, but not eternal. This new rule stated that God would make you suffer for your sins *even if you confessed them.* The degree of suffering would be determined by the severity of the "venial" sin. Control was re-established, Church attendance was up, and collections went up because the doctrine of Purgatory included a way to *buy your way out of suffering...special indulgences!* Indulgences could be granted by an official of the church to free one from the suffering in Purgatory that they had "earned" with their sins. And for a really big contribution, one could obtain a plenary indulgence...a nonstop ticket to heaven. The amount of money, jewels, and land given to the Church in exchange for these plenary indulgences was enormous, equating to literally *millions* of dollars in today's currency. Martin Luther was so outraged by this practice that he created a major schism in the Church in his denunciation of Pope Leo X's "imprimatur" of approval of this practice.

But another problem arose. Plenary indulgences were only for the rich. The masses were frustrated, so they lost faith in the system. Solution? Novena candles. Lighting a certain number of candles and reciting a certain set of prayers would knock years off the sentence of loved ones suffering in Purgatory. In elementary school, the nuns taught us to recite a prayer for a poor soul in Purgatory every time we heard a ringing in our ears...the soul was ringing a bell for a prayer. Funny thing...I *still* say a prayer when my ears ring!

So, now a lot of money was being dropped into candle boxes in an attempt to get God to ease up on the suffering He was inflicting on the souls in Purgatory.

This entire scenario would be funny if it were not true. But it is.

Regardless of the historical support for or against the belief in reincarnation, let's stop to consider just the *logic* behind a one-lifetime scenario. Given the age of the Universe, one lifetime is an infinitesimally short period. One lifetime to make all the mistakes we would inevitably make, then hope for the best at the end. It makes no sense. It doesn't make sense to the Church, either. That's why we continually hear clerics proclaim, "The Lord works in mysterious ways." In other words, don't attempt to make sense of it.

But if "God created man in his own image" as recorded in Genesis, then it only makes sense that God would create and experience who He is through us lifetime after lifetime as we continually evolve towards perfection. "Be ye therefore perfect, even as your Father which is in heaven is perfect" proclaims St. Matthew in 5:48.

The soul's greatest desire is to experience higher and higher aspects of itself, until it reaches enlightenment...total Oneness with God. Without reincarnation, the soul would have to accomplish everything it seeks to accomplish within one lifetime, which is a billion times shorter than the blink of an eye on the cosmic clock.

Once we accept the reality of a series of lifetimes experienced as part of a Divine plan that beckons us towards perfection, can we ever envision a time when our journey is complete? Even when our quest eventually triumphs in our complete reunification with our Creator, is the journey over? I can't even speculate on the nature of an existence after reunification. But if the Creator's Love is creation's fuel, then existence in whatever form, fueled by Love and governed by Divine purpose, would *never* reach a state of completion. We are destined to evolve eternally!

I've grown to believe that our lifetimes on Earth are only a minuscule prelude to a future existence characterized by an inconceivable degree of fulfillment to be earned by our ability to function effortlessly as enlightened stewards of

God's plan. And I believe this plan has no grand conclusion…that *eternity* is everything it's cracked up to be!

Eternity. I mentioned in the Introduction that I get shivers up my spine when I contemplate eternity for more than a few moments. Try it. Close your eyes and think of endlessness…of millions and billions of years of existence and beyond. As linear thinking creatures, we are imprinted with the inevitability of a beginning and an end. We hope for immortality, but cringe at the implications as perceived by our myopic vision of the cosmic plan. We've grown accustomed to struggling to get through *this* lifetime, holding out for the promise of tranquility and perhaps a cold beer at the end of it all.

But now that we've taken a few steps in this book beyond this premise…we've discovered that we live in an enormous Universe existing for perhaps 14 billion years and anticipated to continue for billions more. We've started to consider the possibility that God's grand plan for us may encompass more involvement than a mere 100 years out of this multi-billion year extravaganza. *I hope the whispers are becoming louder.* And this extravaganza, despite our dearth of knowledge of the complete program, should already be generating excitement over the prospects of serving God as a fulfilled sentinel. It's almost as if life just *begins* with enlightenment instead of enlightenment marking the venture's completion.

But why is this possibility so foreign to so many? The answer is patterning. Through the centuries, we have struggled just to have enough to eat and a roof over our heads. Anything else was icing on the cake, and there wasn't much cake! Survival was the name of the game. It became the *reason* for living rather than a means to a greater end. This collective conditioning almost completely overshadowed a higher purpose. That's why Saviors periodically incarnate on Earth, to remove this perceptual logjam. However, religious dogma quickly replaces the true *spiritual* message of the Savior and the process of limitation continues.

But the shadows are fading. Our ability as a society to amass great material prosperity has demonstrated only too clearly that wealth does not automatically equate with happiness. This has been a crucial step in our evolution...it had to precede the transcendence that is crucial to our evolution, as we discussed in previous chapters.

When we are stuck in the survival mode, it is easy to understand the universal appeal of our many fear-and-hope-based religions. So dogma takes a front seat in our survival course.

Chapter 12: Saints and Mysticism

> The goal of human life is the desire to be loved
> by God, to be transformed in and into divine
> Love, and then to become the sacrament of this
> Love and this mystery for others.
>
> Fr. Bede Griffiths

> Direct spiritual experience, is of all means, the
> only direct means of liberation. Liberation is
> never accomplished without it, as sure as food is
> not cooked without heat.
>
> Atmabodha

Although the nature of the subjects covered in this book took shape as the book evolved over the course of many contemplative years, I knew from its inception that one chapter would be dedicated to saints and mysticism.

I'm not referring to saintly emulation. It should be clear by now that the mere mirroring of the good example of saints, commendable as it is, is *not* a path to self-realization.

One of the spiritual classics of the English language is *The Cloud of Unknowing*, originally written in Middle English by an unknown mystic of the 14th century. The author of *The Cloud* has extensive first-hand experience with the mystical. The author explains how all thoughts and concepts must be buried beneath a "cloud of forgetting," while our love must arise toward God hidden in the "cloud of unknowing." The author writes, "With all due reverence, I go so far as to say that it is equally useless to think you can nourish your contemplative work by considering God's attributes... thinking about our Lady, the angels or the saints; or joys of heaven, wonderful as these will be. Of course, it is laudable to reflect upon God's kindness and to love and praise him for it; yet it is far better to let your mind rest in the awareness of him." The "contemplative" method referred to by the author is a means to transcend the typical discourse of prayer and mere mental imagery.

My attraction to saints and their mystical experiences is derived from the remarkable *consistency* of their descriptions of direct communion with the Divine, despite their widely varied religious allegiances. (However, it is important to note that descriptions of religious ecstasy are influenced by the culture within which they occur, including the beliefs and psychology of the recipient.)

In addition, I find their descriptions of Godly communion simply delicious. I periodically taste this meal during my own meditations and, thus, find their descriptions acting as a beckoning to want to experience more and more.

Even a cursory examination of the major religious influences in the world reveals the common thread of mysticism as the heart of their understanding. Hinduism can be traced back to the rishis or mystics of Indian antiquity. Buddhism had its beginnings in the enlightenment of Siddhartha Gautama, the Buddha. Judaism was born out of a process of Divine revelation from God to Abraham, Isaac, Jacob, Moses and the prophets.

It is the same with Christianity and Islam. The Christian tradition rests on Jesus' awareness of His relationship with the Father, and Mohammed encountered Allah through the mediation of the Archangel Gabriel. All these religious traditions emerge out of mystical experience. Mystical experience means a direct knowledge of and relationship with the Divine, God, or unbounded consciousness. I'm even tempted to say that the real religion of mankind isn't religion at all, but rather a mystical spirituality, the womb out of which the religions themselves have been born.

The word "mysticism" often conjures up images of God intoxicated saints. And history reminds us that these "intoxicated" saints were often subject to severe chastisement, excommunication and even death by their superiors. Even today, mainstream religious practice relegates such experiences and their practitioners to the realm of the spiritual ghetto. Obedience to external religious law versus fidelity to one's inner promptings still retains its authoritative position in most religious hierarchies, although I can appreciate the pitfalls of listening exclusively to an inner voice without benefit of an ecclesiastical frame of reference. G. K. Chesterton ridiculed it as the FIF (funny interior feeling) and that "when Jones obeys the inner light, Jones obeys Jones."... a legitimate point. However, the realization of cosmic consciousness or enlightenment spontaneously negates the need for any external validation. At this stage, perfect adherence to natural or Divine law is automatic and self-evident.

Mysticism should not be equated with mystery. It is simply the awakening to and cultivation of transcendental consciousness. This book's essential nature deals with the awakening and cultivation of that transcendental consciousness and the discovery and experience of the transcendental nature of God. And, as I've already stated, I'm an ardent proponent of the ability of the TM-Sidhi Program to rapidly accomplish this cosmic objective. As I wrote in Chapter 7, I not aware of any other modality focused on developing consciousness that exceeds TM's systematic, effortless nature. The TM technique is rooted in the timeless tradition of the ancient Vedas, where the fundamental knowledge was originally cognized directly from the field of Being by enlightened sages while immersed in a superconscious state. There is absolutely no doubt in my mind that the TM-Sidhi Program represents the very highest knowledge available to mankind at this time to awaken and culture transcendental consciousness in our nervous system.

Mystical consciousness means integration with transcendental consciousness and knowing it directly, though it remains beyond adequate description. In fact, many writings on mysticism attempt to explain this experience by explaining what it *isn't*. Words rooted in relativity simply cannot be expected to describe the non-relative. It can be experienced but not fully comprehended. "Under the penalty of words which fail everywhere and communicate nothing but antithesis" proclaims one mystic. But the wisdom of the experience has a practical utility for our spiritual life, including deep peace, joy, compassion, patience, gentleness, selflessness and simplicity.

Although the mystics tend to reflect a commonality of experiences, their paths to the experiences can be quite different. The chronicles of these paths range from severe ascetic practices, devout prayer, fasting, meditation, and direct Divine intercession, or a combination of the above. For some, it simply "shows up" with little warning, often causing personal consternation due to the experiencer's lack of a frame of reference. Sometimes the experiencer believes he is going mad. Indeed, some mystics *have* been declared mad due to ignorance of the roots of the experience.

Of course, entire libraries exist on the lives of the saints from the major religious traditions. However, my purpose in composing this chapter on Saints and Mysticism is simply twofold. First, to briefly reveal some of the common descriptions of experiences of specific individuals on the path to transcendental consciousness. And secondly, to emphasize and embrace the fact that "sainthood" is our birthright and the ultimate destination of each one of us! In mystical Christianity, it has been experienced that Divinity pervades everything. It is our task to meet that Spirit within ourselves.

My journey in life thus far leads me no choice but to believe with every fiber of my being that the destination of sainthood can not only be achieved, but that it is inherent in everyone to do so whether we realize it or not. Furthermore, I believe it is our *responsibility* as "owners" of this human frame to honor the Divine within by recognizing that we have this Divine heritage.

Before we proceed to explore specific descriptions of mystical experience, let me emphasize that I'm affording the subject only the most cursory attention. It's merely a taste, albeit a delicious one. Various authors have provided discerning insights into the subject, which I recommend reading. These authors include William Johnston's *The Still Point: Reflections On Zen and Christian Mysticism* and *Silent Music: The Science of Meditation*; *Lamps of Western Mysticism* by Arthur Waite; the classic 14th century text, *The Cloud of Unknowing* (author unknown); Aldous Huxley's *The Perennial Philosophy*; *Ecstatic Confessions* by Martin Buber; and *Conversions*, edited by Hugh Kerr and John Mulder.

The following experiences contain descriptions of beatific visions. However, Jed McKenna, in *Spiritual Enlightenment: The Damnedest Thing*, writes of the importance of understanding "that mystical experiences and enlightenment are not synonymous…it's possible to have one without the other." Additionally, he says, "Samadhi (intense bliss) is the most beautiful and profound experience a human being can hope to have, but it is only of peripheral interest within the context of spiritual awakening."

McKenna is correct. Mystical experiences are only symptoms of a culturing of the nervous system via habitual transcending to experience unbounded awareness. And as the "mystic" continues to experience transcendental consciousness, the experience continues to purify the nervous system until it can maintain unbounded awareness permanently. This is the classical description of enlightenment. However, there are degrees of enlightenment, ranging from the initial permanency of unbounded awareness (often referred to as cosmic consciousness) to complete union with the Divine (unity consciousness). Detailed descriptions of these states can be found in Maharishi Mahesh Yogi's *Science of Being and the Art of Living.*

As I stated, this experience is not the sole domain of a privileged few. It is our common destiny. And why wouldn't our all-Loving Father want it any other way?

Although mystics primarily report the following descriptions from the Christian tradition, the experiences of mystics from all traditions are on the same level as Christianity in its fullness of transforming union (the spiritual marriage between God and the soul). Christianity does not have a monopoly on wisdom as it relates to the nature of the Divine. Christian theological formulations do not exhaust the infinite reality of other forms of spirituality.

It is also important to discuss the common denominator of experience...transcendence. It literally means "going beyond." Going beyond all descriptions...all words. Words existing in the relative field can never sufficiently describe a non-relative experience. This may be a difficult concept to grasp, since most of us are left-brain wired humans in need of concrete frames of reference. But as *The Cloud* author writes, "Only he who experiences it will really understand." The message here is not to explain, but to reach a state of consciousness where we see for ourselves. The author exhorts us to "go after experience rather than knowledge...knowledge may deceive you. Knowledge tends to breed conceit...you must simply sit in mediation."

You may ask... "Exactly where is the Transcendent? It appears to be nowhere." Exactly. Nowhere physically is everywhere spiritually. The *Cloud's* author states:

> No one can possess [God] through knowledge. I prefer to be lost in this nowhere, wrestling with this blind nothingness, than to be like some great lord traveling everywhere and enjoying the world as if he owned it. Forget that kind of everywhere and the world's all. It pales in richness beside this blessed

nothingness and nowhere. Don't worry if your faculties fail to grasp it. Actually, that is the way it should be, for this nothingness is so lofty that they cannot reach it. It cannot be explained, only experienced.

In Chapter 6, Maharishi Mahesh Yogi touched on this idea of nothingness as follows:

When we have transcended the experience of the subtlest object, the experiencer is left by himself without an experience, without an object of experience, and without the process of experiencing. When the subject is left without an object of experience, having transcended the subtlest state of the object, he steps out of the process of experiencing and arrives at the state of Being. The mind is then found in the state of Being which is beyond the relative field.

How is the Transcendent reached? The *Cloud's* author's method of transcending thought is the use of a "sacred word." (A sacred word is referred to as a mantra in eastern philosophy.) The sacred word possesses a special quality or vibration. It is used to clear all images and thoughts from the mind, "leaving it free to love with the blind stirring that stretches out toward God."

If the reader is familiar with the specific approach followed by practitioners of the Transcendental Meditation technique, you will immediately perceive TM's mirroring of the *Cloud's* description of the effortless use of a sacred word to pave the path to the Transcendent. However, my personal experience indicates that the *systematic* component of TM magnifies significantly the intensity, rapidity and consistency of experience of the transcending process. For lack of a better term, TM "standardizes" the process, whereas most mystical traditions and their teachers lack a clear understanding of how to systematically engender the transcending process in order for the practitioner to create the experiences on a routine basis and thus advance much more quickly to the goal.

The following descriptions reflect experiences featuring a fairly common phenomenon... bright light:

Hildegard von Bingen (1099 – 1179):

> That light that I see is not local; it is far, far brighter than the cloud that carries the sun...And it is called by me the shadow of the living light.

Sophia von Klingnau...14th century:

> I saw that a light, beautiful and blissful beyond measure, was coming from heaven, and it surrounded me and shone through me and illuminated me entirely, and my heart was transformed all of a sudden and filled with an unspeakable and strange joy, so that I utterly and completely forgot all the misery and torment that I had ever known until this time. And what marvels I saw...all humans together could not put into words.

Charles Finney (1792 – 1875):

> All at once the glory of God shone upon and round about me...A light perfectly ineffable shone in my soul, and almost prostrated me on the ground...This light seemed like the brightness of the sun in every direction. It was too intense for the eyes...No words can express the wonderful love that was shed abroad in my heart. I wept aloud with joy and love.

Mrs. Jonathan Edwards 18th century:

> ...and I appeared to myself to float or swim, in these bright sweet beams, like motes swimming in the beams of the sun, or the streams of light which come in at the window.

R.M. Bucke (Canadian psychiatrist):

All at once...I found myself wrapped in a flame-colored cloud...I knew the fire was within myself...there came upon me a sense of exultation, of immense joyousness accompanied and immediately followed by an intellectual illumination impossible to describe...I saw that the universe...is...a living Presence...and (I saw) that the happiness of each and all is in the long run absolutely certain.

Anna Katharina Emmerich (1774 – 1824):

I usually see first a brightness, and then a form suddenly emerges shining from the night.

The following descriptions reflect profound experiences of *union* with the Divine. The experiences are also very difficult, if not impossible, to put into words. Most practitioners expressing a union connection believe it is a far more important and valid experience than the more peripheral experience of light:

Lady Julian of Norwich...recorded in 1373:

It is a high knowledge to see inwardly and to know that God, who is our creator, dwells in our soul. And it is a higher and more inner knowledge to see and to know that our soul...dwells essentially in God.

Teresa of Avila (1515 – 1582):

In the orison of union, the soul is fully awake as regards God, but wholly asleep as regards things of this world and in respect to oneself. God establishes himself in the interior of this soul in such a way, that when I return to it, it is wholly impossible to doubt that I have been in God, and God in me.

Jacob Boehme (1575 – 1624):

In one quarter of an hour I saw and knew more than if I had been many years together at a university. For I saw and knew the being of all things.

Thomas Merton (1915 – 1968):

> The whole illusion of a separate holy existence is a dream...There is no way of telling people that they are all walking around shining like the sun...Then it was as if I suddenly saw the secret beauty of their hearts, the depths of their hearts where neither sin nor desire...can reach...the person that each one is in God's eyes. If only they could see themselves as they really are. If only we could see each other that way all the time. There would be no more war, no more hatred, no more cruelty, no more greed...I suppose the big problem would be that we would fall down and worship each other. But this cannot be seen, only believed and understood.

Continuing this union theme, Eckhart writes:

> The knower and the known are one. Simple people imagine that they should see God, as if He stood there and they here. This is not so. God and I, we are one in knowledge. All that the imagination can imagine and the reason conceive and understand in this life is not, and cannot be, a proximate means of union with God.

Eckhart also writes of a Sister Katrei's conversations with her confessor where the confessor asks her, "Let me enjoy divine faithfulness; reveal to me what you have experienced." She replied:

> God knows I cannot. What I have experienced, no one can put into words...When I looked into myself, I saw God in myself and everything God ever created in heaven and earth...You should know that all that is put into words and presented to people with images is nothing but a stimulus to God. Know that in God there is nothing but God. Know that no soul can enter into God unless it first becomes God just as it was before it was created.

Else von Neustadt, 13th – 14th century, when asked about her vision:

> It is a divine vision, of which no one can say anything except the one who sees it, and even those who see it cannot speak of it rightly...God is in me and I in him; he is mine and I am his; he belongs to me and I to him.

The importance of entering into this practice with effortlessness is also a consistent theme. We often think of contemplation or meditation as a concentration practice requiring long, arduous hours of performance over the course of many years before these experiences materialize. However, the opposite is true. The key is effortlessness. The use of the sacred word or mantra has a quality associated with it that gently advances the practitioner to follow this path of least resistance.

St. Francois de Sales wrote:

> If the heart wonders or is distracted, bring it back to the point quite gently and replace it tenderly in its Master's presence. And even if you did nothing during the whole of your hour but bring your heart back and place it again in Our Lord's presence, though it went away every time you brought it back, your hour would be very well employed.

The author of *The Cloud* sharply admonishes those who attempt to reason and discourse when the time for silent contemplation has come:

> When contemplation is born, reason dies; Comtemplatives who endeavor to think only kill their incipient mystical life.

Finally, it is important to note that a hallmark of a mystic's life is *integration* with activity and not a permanent retreat into the void. A true mystic demonstrates an organic growth, reflecting the beauty of the transcendent into daily life. Teresa of Avila would not have cared about a mystic's EEG scores. Rather, she would have asked about his adaptability to community living, her humble service to others, his habits of hard work and her ability to do drudgery.

And so with the above thoughts on *integration* in mind, we end this book by returning to the beginning…

> One day a student asked, "Master, what work should an adherent perform prior to being blessed with Enlightenment?" The wise Master responded, "Chop wood, carry water."

> The inquisitive student then asked, "Master, what does a perfected man do *after* attaining Enlightenment?" The Master, looking at the student with a wry smile, replied, "Chop wood, carry water."